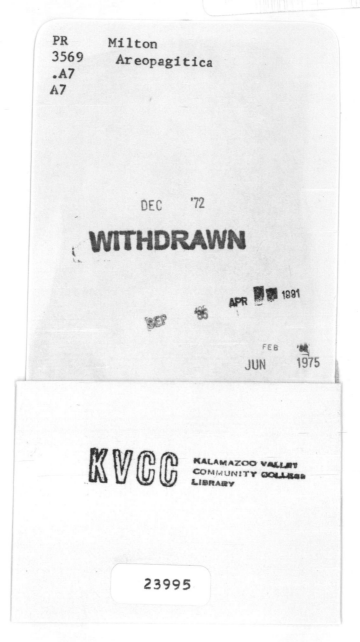

JOHN MILTON.

AREOPAGITICA.

[24 November] 1644.

PRECEDED BY ILLUSTRATIVE DOCUMENTS.

CAREFULLY EDITED BY

EDWARD ARBER,

Affociate, King's College, London, F.R.G.S., &c.

Albert Saifer

Philadelphia   1972

English Reprints.

JOHN MILTON.

AREOPAGITICA.

[24 November] 1644.

PRECEDED BY ILLUSTRATIVE DOCUMENTS.

CAREFULLY EDITED BY

EDWARD ARBER,

Associate, King's College, London, F.R.G.S., &c.

LONDON :
ALEX. MURRAY & SON, 30, QUEEN SQUARE, W.C.
1 January, 1868

Ext. Stat. Hall.] SIXPENCE. [*All Rights reserved.*

CONTENTS.

AREOPAGITICA.[1]

INTRODUCTION.

HAT half-living thing—a book : may be re-garded in many ways. It may be confidered in connection with the circumftances which led to its conception and creation ; and in the midft of which it appeared. It may be ftudied, as exhibiting the moral intent, the mental power of its author. Its contents may be analyfed as to their intrinfic truthfulnefs or falfity. We may trace and identify its influence upon its own age and on fucceeding generations. This is an apprehenfion of the mind of a book.

More than this. We may examine its ftyle, its power and manner of expreffing that mind. The ringing collocation of its words, the harmonious cadence of its fentences, the flafhing gem-like beauty of ifolated paffages, the juft mapping out of the general argument, the due fubordination of its feveral parts, their final inweaving into one overpowering conclufion : thefe are the features, difcovering, illuminating, enforcing the mind of a book.

Much of what is in books is falfe, much only half true, much true. It is impoffible to feparate the tares from the wheat. Every one, therefore—of neceffity—muft read difcriminatively ; often fifting and fearching for firft principles, often tefting the catenation of an argument, often treafuring up incidental truths for future ufe ; enjoying—as delights by the way—whatever felicity of expreffion, gorgeoufnefs of imagination, vividnefs of defcription, or aptnefs of illuftration may glance, like funfhine, athwart the path : the journey's end being Truth.

The purpofe through thefe Englifh Reprints is to bring this modern age face to face with the works of our forefathers. The Editor and his clumfy framework

are unimportant and may be forgotten ; if but that
the attention may be riveted upon the picture. The
thought of thefe Englifh Writers is not dead.   It
flumbers.   Underftand and then fubtract from it, the
local colouring of time and circumftance, and it is
inftinct with life : either the noxious life of foul
delufive error, or the ethereal life of Truth.   We
have not, as yet, in all things attained to the height
of our Predeceffors' far-feeing conception : and even
the juft meafuring of their many miftakes and errors
may not be time and effort thrown away.

While there is very much for us to learn from our
Ancients, both in what they faid and their manner of
faying it; there bids fair to be an increafing number
of learners among the Moderns.   England is on the
eve of a great Education, in the which the unlettered
will become readers, the readers ftudents, the ftudents
fcholars.   With this wider variety and increafed
power of the Englifh mind, the diligent ftudy of the
national Literature and Language can hardly fail
both to fpread and to deepen.   The number of fuch
learners tends therefore to multiply, until it fhall be
reputed a difgrace to be ignorant of our mother tongue
and of that which it enfhrines.

There is alfo no better or more effential preparative
for the outcome of a glorious literature in the Future,
than the careful ftudy and accurate appreciation of
the treafures of the Paft.   The prefent Merchant-
Adventurer will efteem the ' Englifh Reprints ' to be
crowned with a happy fuccefs ; if—bringing thofe
treafures, as from afar, to every one's home, and there
difplaying them to a more public gaze—they fhall, in
however infignificant a degree, tend to that happy End.

The Printing Prefs, among many advantages, brought
to its early poffeffors one conftant perplexity, which,
however, affumed different forms to different minds.
The power of every man, of every educated man, was
by it immenfely increafed for good or for evil.   The

true-hearted grieved over the facility the prefs gave to the fpread of error. The high-bred defpot chafed at the new power ceafeleffly exercifed by the low-bred intellect in queftioning and adjufting his prerogative, in deftroying his would-be almightinefs in the mind of the people, in bringing him under Law. The minifters of the religions then extant were alarmed at the ready promulgation of those reftlefs inquiries into the ulti- mate nature of all things, left they fhould undermine the foundations of civil fociety and ecclefiaftical polity, and fo reduce the world to chaotic confufion. Thus fome from confcientious duty, others with a wicked fatisfaction, all unitedly or in turn, joined in clogging the Prefs, in curtailing the new power that God in His Providence had beftowed upon mankind.

Dr. Johnfon, in his *Life of Milton*—which, either for wilful mifreprefentation or crafs incapacity to ap- preciate his fubject, is to his perpetual difcredit—fairly reprefents the views of one fide on the Liberty of the Prefs, and through that the boundlefs liberty of human thought.

" The danger of fuch unbounded liberty, and the danger of bounding it, have produced a problem in the fcience of Govern- ment which human underftanding feems hitherto unable to folve. If nothing may be publifhed but what civil authority fhall have previoufly approved, power muft always be the ftandard of truth ; if every dreamer of innovations may propagate his pro- jects, there can be no fettlement ; if every murmurer at govern- ment may diffufe difcontent, there can be no peace ; and if every fceptick in theology may teach his follies, there can be no reli- gion. The remedy againft thefe evils is to punifh the authors ; for it is yet allowed that every fociety may punifh, though not prevent, the publication of opinions, which that fociety fhall think pernicious ; but this punifhment, though it may crufh the author, promotes the book ; and it feems not more reafonable to leave the right of printing unreftrained, becaufe writers may be afterwards cenfured, than it would be to fleep with doors unbolted, becaufe by our laws we can hang a thief." *

Milton's anfwer to this had been already written:— " Give me the liberty to know, to utter, and to argue freely according to confcience above all liberties. † . . . Though all

* *Lives of English Poets,* I., 153, 154. London, 1781.   † p. 73.

the windes of doctrin were let loose to play upon the earth, so Truth be in the field, we do injuriously by licencing and pro- hibiting to misdoubt her strengh. Let her and Falshood grapple; who ever knew Truth put to the wors, in a free and open en- counter. Her confuting is the best and surest supressing. . . . . Who knows not that Truth is strong next to the Almighty; she needs no policies, no stratagems, no licencings to make her vic- torious, those are the shifts and the defences that error uses against her power."*

As we learn from ʰis *Second Defence*—written ten years after the present work—the singularly conceptive mind of Milton had grouped into one cycle subjects of no apparent immediate connection. Episcopacy, Divorce, Education, Freedom of the Individual, Free- dom of the Press, had, to his mind, one point of iden- tity and contact, one connecting link,—Liberty. This, a cardinal thought of his entire life, seems to have almost overpowered him, as he saw the break-up of the system of the *Thorough*, the nation uprising against the tyranny of a few, and laying—for all coming ages —the foundations of that religious, civil, and domestic Liberty, which it is our happiness to enjoy.

Of that great cycle, the 'Areopagitica' occupies but a subordinate part, Milton classifying it under domestic liberty with divorce and education.   He there also tells us, his purpose in writing it :—

" I wrote my Areopagitica, in order to deliver the press from the restraints with which it was encumbered ; that the power of determining what was true and what was false, what ought to be published and what to be suppressed, might no longer be en- trusted to a few illiterate and illiberal individuals, who refused their sanction to any work which contained views or sentiments at all above the level of the vulgar superstition."†

The following Orders, &c., have been reprinted ; partly to give the groundwork of fact to Milton's argu- ment ; partly to show the strong hand and the blunt mind of our Ancestors in respect to the Press ; and partly to assist to a more perfect realization of the an- tagonistic ideas and circumstances, in the midst of which, Milton conceived the 'Areopagitica,' and so to render more apparent its beauty and originality.

* p. 74.   † *Prose Works*, I., 259: St. John's Ed., 1848.

A

DECREE

OF

Starre-Chamber,

CONCERNING

PRINTING,

Made the eleuenth day of July last past. 1637.

⁋ Imprinted at London by *Robert Barker*
Printer to the Kings most Excellent
Maiestie : And by the Assignes
of *Iohn Bill.* 1637.

In Camera Stellata coram Concilio ibidem, vndecimo die
Iulij, Anno decimo tertio
CAROLI *Regis.*

His day Sir Iohn Bankes *Knight, His Maiesties Attourney Generall, produced in Court a Decree drawn and penned by the aduice of the Right Honourable the* Lord Keeper *of the great Seale of England, the most Reuerend Father in God the Lord* Arch-Bishop of Canterbury his Grace, *the Right Honorable and Right Reuerend Father in God the Lord* Bishop of London Lord high Treasurer of England, *the* Lord chiefe Iustices, *and the* Lord chiefe Baron, *touching the regulating of Printers and Founders of letters, whereof the Court hauing consideration, the said Decree was directed and ordered to be here Recorded, and to the end the same may be publique, and that euery one whom it may concerne may take notice thereof, The Court hath now also ordered, That the said Decree shall speedily be Printed, and that the same be sent to His* Maiesties *Printer for that purpose. Whereas the three and twentieth day of Iune in the eight ana twentieth yere of the reigne of the late Queene* Elizabeth, *ana before, diuers Decrees and Ordinances haue beene made for the better gouernment and regulating of Printers ana Printing, which Orders and Decrees haue beene found by experience to be defectiue in some particulars; Ana diuers abuses have sithence arisen, and beene practised by the craft and malice of wicked and euill disposed persons, to the preiudice of the publike; And diuers libellous, seditious, and mutinous bookes haue beene vnduly printed, and other bookes and papers without licence, to the disturbance of the peace of the Church and State: For preuention whereof in time to come, It is now Ordered and Decreed, That the said former Decrees and Ordinances shall stand in force with these Additions, Explanations, and Alterations following,* viz.

In Camera Stellata coram Con-
cilio ibidem, vndecimo die Iulii,
Anno decimo tertio CAROLI
Regis.

Mprimis, That no perfon or perfons whatfoeuer fhall prefume to print, or caufe to
bee printed, either in the parts beyond
the Seas, or in this Realme, or other his
Maiefties Dominions, any feditious, fcifma-
ticall, or offenfive Bookes or Pamphlets, to the fcandall
of Religion, or the Church, or the Government, or
Governours of the Church or State, or Commonwealth,
or of any Corporation, or particular perfon or perfons
whatfoeuer, nor fhall import any fuch Booke or Bookes,
nor fell or difpofe of them, or any of them, nor caufe
any fuch to be bound, ftitched, or fowed, vpon paine
that he or they fo offending, fhall loofe all fuch Bookes
and Pamphlets, and alfo haue, and fuffer fuch correction,
and fevere punifhment, either by Fine, imprifonment,
or other corporall punifhment, or otherwife, as by this
Court, or by His Maiefties Commifsioners for caufes
Ecclefiafticall in the high Commifsion Court, refpectiuely, as the feveral caufes fhall require, fhall be
thought fit to be inflicted upon him, or them, for fuch
their offence and contempt.

II. *Item*, That no perfon or perfons whatfoeuer,
fhall at any time print or caufe to be imprinted, any
Booke or Pamphlet whatfoever, vnleffe the fame Booke

or Pamphlet, and alfo all and euery the Titles, Epiftles, Prefaces, Proems, Preambles, Introductions, Tables, Dedications, and other matters and things whatfoeuer thereunto annexed, or therewith imprinted, fhall be firft lawfully licenced and authorized onely by fuch perfon and perfons as are hereafter expreffed, and by no other, and fhall be also firft entred into the Regifters Booke of the Company of Stationers ; vpon paine that euery Printer offending therein, fhall be for euer hereafter difabled to ufe or exercife the Art or Myfterie of Printing, and receiue fuch further punifhment, as by this Court or the high Commifsion Court refpectiuely, as the feverall caufes fhall require, fhall be thought fitting.

III. *Item*, That all Bookes concerning the common Lawes of this Realme fhall be printed by the efpeciall allowance of the Lords chiefe Iuftices, and the Lord chiefe Baron for the time being, or one or more of them, or by their appointment ; And that all Books of Hiftory, belonging to this State, and prefent times, or any other Booke of State affaires, fhall be licenced by the principall Secretaries of State, or one of them, or by their appointment ; And that all Bookes concerning Heraldry, Titles of Honour and Armes, or otherwife concerning the Office of Earle Marfhall, fhall be licenced by the Earle Marfhall, or by his appointment ; And further, that all other Books, whether of Diuinitie, Phificke, Philofophie, Poetry, or whatfoeuer, fhall be allowed by the Lord Arch-Bifhop of *Canterbury*, or Bifhop of *London* for the time being, or by their appointment, or the Chancellours, or Vice Chancellors of either of the Vinuerfities of this Realme for the time being.

Always prouided, that the Chancellour or Vice-Chancellour, of either of the Vniuerfities, fhall Licence onely fuch Booke or Bookes that are to be Printed within the limits of the Vniuerfities refpectiuely, but not in *London*, or elfewhere, not medling either with Bookes of the common Law, or matters of State.

IV. *Item*, That euery perfon and perfons, which by any Decree of this Court are, or fhall be appointed or

authorized to Licence Bookes, or giue Warrant for im-
printing thereof, as is aforefaid, fhall haue two feuerall
written Copies of the fame Booke or Bookes with the
Titles, Epiftles, Prefaces, Proems, Preambles, Introductions, Tables, Dedications, and other things whatfoeuer thereunto annexed. One of which faid Copies
fhall be kept in the publike Regiftries of the faid Lord
Arch-Bifhop, and Bifhop of *London* refpectiuely, or
in the Office of the Chancellour, or Vice-Chancellour
of either of the Vniuerfities, or with the Earle Marfhall,
or principall Secretaries of State, or with the Lords
chiefe Iuftices, or chiefe Baron, of all fuch Bookes as
fhall be licenfed by them refpectiuely, to the end that
he or they may be fecure, that the Copy fo licenfed by
him or them fhall not bee altered without his or their
priuitie, and the other fhall remain with him whofe
Copy it is, and vpon both the faid Copies, he or they
that fhall allow the faid Booke, fhall teftifie vnder his
or their hand or hands, that there is nothing in that
Booke or Books contained, that is contrary to Chris-
tian Faith, and the Doctrine and Difcipline of the
Church of *England*, nor againft the State or Gouernment, nor contrary to good life, or good manners, or
otherwife, as the nature and fubiect of the work fhall
require, which licenfe or approbation fhall be imprinted in the beginning of the fame Booke, with the
name, or names of him or them that fhall authorize or
licenfe the fame, for a teftimonie of the allowance thereof.

V. *Item*, That every Merchant of bookes, and perfon and perfons whatfoeuer, which doth, or hereafter
fhall buy, or import, or bring any booke or bookes
into this Realme, from any parts beyond the Seas,
fhall before fuch time as the fame book or books, or
any of them be deliuered forth, or out of his, or their
hand or hands, or expofed to fale, giue, and prefent
a true Catalogue in writing of all and euery fuch booke
and bookes vnto the Lord Arch-Bifhop of *Canterbury*,
or Lord Bifhop of *London* for the time being, vpon
paine to haue and fuffer fuch punifhment for offending

herein, as by this Court, or by the faid high Commifsion Court refpectiuely, as the feueral caufes fhall
require, fhall be thought fitting.

VI. *Item*, That no Merchant, or other perfon or
perfons whatfoeuer, which fhall import or bring any
book or books into the kingdome, from any parts
beyond the Seas, fhall prefume to open any Dry-fats,
Bales, Packs, Maunds, or other Fardals of books, or
wherein books are; nor fhall any Searcher, Wayter, or
other Officer belonging to the Cuftome-houfe, vpon
pain of loofing his or ·their place or places, fuffer the
fame to paffe, or to be deliuered out of their hands or
cuftody, before fuch time as the Lord Arch-Bifhop of
Canterbury, or Lord Bifhop of *London*, or one of them
for the time being, haue appointed one of their Chaplains, or fome other learned man, with the Mafter and
Wardens ² of the Company of Stationers, or one of
them, and fuch others as they fhall call to their afsiftance, to be prefent at the opening thereof, and to view
the fame: And if there fhall happen to be found
any feditious, fchifmaticall or offenfiue booke or
bookes, they fhall forthwith be brought vnto the faid
Lord Arch-bifhop of *Canterbury*, Lord Bifhop of *London*
for the time being, or one of them, or to the High
Commifsion Office, to the end that as well the offendor
or offendors may be punifhed by the Court of Star
Chamber, or the high Commifsion Court refpectiuely,
as the feuerall caufes fhall require, according to his or
their demerit; as alfo that fuch further courfe and
order may be taken concerning the fame booke or
bookes, as fhall bee thought fitting.

VII. *Item*, That no perfon or perfons fhall within
this Kingdome, or elfewhere imprint, or caufe to be imprinted, nor fhall import or bring in, or caufe to be
imported or brought into this Kingdome, from, or out
of any other His Maiefties Dominions, nor from other,
or any parts beyond the Seas, any Copy, book or
books, or part of any booke or bookes, printed beyond
the feas, or elfewhere, which the faid Company of

Stationers, or any other perfon or perfons haue, or fhall by any Letters Patents, Order, or Entrance in their Regifter book, or otherwife, haue the right, priuiledge, authoritie, or allowance foly to print, nor fhall bind, ftitch, or put to fale, any fuch booke or bookes, vpon paine of loffe and forfeiture of all the faid. bookes, and of fuch Fine, or other punifhment, for euery booke or part of a booke fo imprinted or imported, bound, ftitched, or put to fale, to be leyued of the party fo offending, as by the power of this Court, or the high Commiffion Court refpectiuely, as the feverall caufes fhall require, fhall be thought fit.

VIII. *Item*, Euery perfon and perfons that fhall hereafter Print, or caufe to be Printed, any Bookes, Ballads, Charts, Portraiture, or any other thing or things whatfoeuer, fhall thereunto or thereon Print and fet his and their owne name or names, as alfo the name or names of the Author or Authors, Maker or Makers of the fame, and by, or for whom any fuch booke, or other thing is, or fhall be printed, vpon pain of forfiture of all fuch Books, Ballads, Chartes, Portraitures, and other thing or things, printed contrary to this Article; And the preffes, Letters and other inftruments for Printing, wherewith fuch Books, ballads, Chartes, Portraitures, and other thing or things fhall be printed, to be defaced and made vnferuiceable, and the party and parties fo offending, to be fined, imprifoned and haue fuch other corporall punifhment, or otherwife, as by this Honourable Court, or the faid high Commiffion refpectiuely, as the feuerall caufes fhall require, fhall be thought fit.

IX. *Item*, That no perfon or perfons whatfoeuer, fhall hereafter print, or caufe to be printed, or fhall forge, put, or counterfeit in, or vpon any booke or books, the name, title, marke or vinnet of the Company or Society of Stationers, or of any particular perfon or perfons, which hath or fhall haue lawfull priuiledge, authoritie, or allowance to print the fame, without the confent of the faid Company, or party or parties that are or fhall be fo priuiledged, authorized, or allowed to print the fame booke or books, thing or things, firft had and obtained, vpon paine that euery perfon or perfons fo offending, fhall not onely loofe all fuch books and other things, but fhall alfo haue, and fuffer fuch punifhment, by imprifonment of his body, fine, or otherwife, as by this Honourable Court, or high Commifsion Court refpectiuely, as the feuerall caufes fhall require, it fhall be to him or them limited or adiudged.

X. *Item*, that no Haberdafher of fmall wares, Ironmonger, Chandler, Shop-keeper, or any other perfon or perfons whatfoeuer, not hauing beene feuen yeeres apprentice to the trade of a Book-feller, Printer, or Book-binder, fhall within the citie or fuburbs of London, or in any other Corporation, Market-towne, or elfwhere, receive, take or buy, to barter, fell againe, change or do away any Bibles, Teftaments, Pfalm-books, Primers, Abcees, Almanackes, or other booke or books whatfoeuer, vpon pain of forfeiture of all fuch books fo receiued, bought or taken as aforefaid, and fuch other punifhme.it of the parties fo offending, as by this Court, or the faid high Commifsion Court refpectiuely, as the feverall caufes fhall require, fhall be thought meet.

XI. *Item*, for that Printing is, and for many yeers hath been an Art and manufacture of this kingdome, for the better incouraging of Printers in their honeft, and iuft endeauours in their profefsion, and preuention of diuers libels, pamphlets, and feditious books printed beyond the feas in Englifh, and thence trans-ported hither ;

It is further Ordered and Decreed, that no Mer-chant, Bookfeller, or other perfon or perfons whatfoeuer, fhall imprint, or caufe to be imprinted, in the parts beyond the feas or elfwhere, nor fhall import or bring, nor willingly afsift or confent to the importation or bringing from beyond the feas into this Realme, any Englifh bookes, or part of bookes, or bookes what-foeuer, which are or fhall be, or the greater or more part whereof is or fhall be Englifh, or of the Englifh tongue, whether the fame book or bookes haue been here formerly printed or not, vpon pain of the forfeiture of all fuch Englifh bookes fo imprinted or imported, and fuch further cenfure and punifhment, as by this Court, or the faid high Commifsion Court refpectiuely, as the feuerall caufes fhall require, fhall be thought meet.

XII. *Item*, That no ftranger or forreigner whatfoeuer, be fuffered to bring in, or vent here, any booke or bookes printed beyond the feas, in any language whatfoeuer, either by themfelues or their fecret Factors, except fuch onely as bee free Stationers of *London*, and fuch as haue beene brought vp in that profefsion, and haue their whole meanes of fubfiftance, and liuelihood depending thereupon, vpon paine of confifcation of all fuch Books fo imported, and fuch further penalties, as by this Court, or the high Commifsion Court refpectiuely, as the feuerall caufes fhall require, fhall be thought fit to be impofed.

XIII. *Item*, That no perfon or perfons within the Citie of *London*, or the liberties thereof, or elfewhere, fhall erect or caufe to be erected any Preffe or Printing-houfe, nor fhall demife, or let, or fuffer to be held or vfed, any houfe, vault, feller, or other roome whatfoeuer, to, or by any perfon or perfons, for a Printing-houfe, or place to print in, vnlefse he or they which fhall fo demife or let the fame, or fuffer the fame to be fo vfed, fhall firft giue notice to the faid Mafter and Wardens of the Company of Stationers for the time being, of fuch demife, or fuffering to worke or print there, vpon paine of imprifonment, and fuch other punifhment as by this Court, or the faid high Commifsion Court refpectiuely, as the feuerall Caufes fhall require, fhall bee thought fit.

XIV. *Item*, That no Ioyner, or Carpenter, or other perfon, fhall make any printing-Preffe, no Smith fhall forge any Iron-worke for a printing-Preffe, and no Founder fhall caft any Letters for any perfon or perfons whatfoeuer, neither fhall any perfon or perfons bring, or caufe to be brought in from any parts beyond

the Seas, any Letters Founded or Caſt, nor buy any
ſuch Letters for Printing, Vnleſſe he or they reſpectiuely ſhall firſt acquaint the ſaid Maſter and Wardens,
or ſome of them, for whom the ſame Preſſe, Iron-works,
or Letters, are to be made, forged, or caſt, vpon paine
of ſuch fine and puniſhment, as this Court, or the high
Commiſsion Court reſpectiuely, as the feuerall cauſes
ſhall require, ſhall thinke fit.

XV. *Item*, The Court doth declare, that as formerly,
ſo now, there ſhall be but Twentie Maſter Printers
allowed to haue the vſe of one Preſſe or more, as is
after ſpecified, and doth hereby nominate, allow, and
admit theſe perſons whoſe names hereafter follow, to
the number of Twentie, to have the vſe of a Preſſe, or
Preſſes and Printing-houſe, for the time being, *viz. Felix
Kingſtone, Adam Iſlip, Thomas Purfoot, Miles Fleſher,
Thomas Harper, Iohn Beale, Iohn Legat, Robert Young,
Iohn Haviland, George Miller, Richard Badger, Thomas
Cotes, Bernard Alſop, Richard Biſhop, Edward Griffin,
Thomas Purſlow, Richard Hodgkinſonne, Iohn Dawſon,
Iohn Raworth, Marmaduke Parſons.* And further, th̃
Court doth order and decree, That it ſhall be lawfull for
the Lord Arch-Biſhop of *Canterbury*, or the Lord
Biſhop of *London*, for the time being, taking to him or
them ſix other high Commiſsioners, to ſupply the place
or places of thoſe which are now already Printers by this
Court, as they ſhall fall void by death, or Cenſure, or
otherwiſe : Prouided that they exceed not the number
of Twentie, beſides His Maieſties Printers, and the
Printers allowed for the Vniuerſities.

XVI. *Item*, That euery perſon or perſons, now allowed or admitted to have the vſe of a Preſſe, and
Printing-houſe, ſhall within Ten dayes after the date
hereof, become bound with ſureties to His Maieſtie in
the high Commiſsion Court, in the ſum of three hun-
dred pounds, not to print or ſuffer to be printed in his
houſe or Preſſe, any booke, or bookes whatſoeuer, but
ſuch as ſhall from time to time be lawfully licenſed,
and that the like Bond ſhall be entred into by all, and
euery perſon and perſons, that hereafter ſhall be admit-

ted, or allowed to print, before he or they be fuffered to haue the vfe of a Preffe.

XVII. *Item*, That no allowed Printer fhall keep aboue two Preffes, vnleffe he hath been Mafter or vpper Warden[2] of his Company, who are thereby allowed to keep three Preffes and no more, vnder paine of being difabled for euer after to keepe or vfe any Preffe at all, vnleffe for fome great and fpecial occafion for the publique, he or they haue for a time leaue of the Lord Arch-Bifhop of *Canterbury*, or Lord Bifhop of *London* for the time being, to have or vfe one, or more aboue the forefaid number, as their Lordfhips, or either of them fhall thinke fit. And whereas there are fome Mafter Printers that haue at this prefent one, or more Preffes allowed them by this Decree, the Court doth further order and declare, That the Mafter and Wardens of the Company of Stationers, doe foorthwith certifie the Lord Arch-Bifhop of *Canterbury*, or the Lord Bifhop of *London*, what number of Preffes each Mafter Printer hath, that their Lordfhips or either of them, taking vnto them fix other high Commiffioners, may take fuch prefent order for the fuppreffing of the fupernumerarie Preffes, as to their Lordfhips, or to either of them fhall feem beft.

XVIII. *Item*, That no perfon or perfons, do hereafter reprint, or caufe to be reprinted, any booke or bookes whatfoeuer (though formerly printed with licence) without being reuiewed, and a new Licence obtained for the reprinting thereof. Alwayes provided, that the Stationer or Printer be put to no other charge hereby, but the bringing and leauing of two printed copies of the book to be printed, as is before expreffed of written Copies, with all fuch additions as the Author hath made.

XIX. *Item*, The Court doth declare, as formerly, fo now, That no Apprentices be taken into any printing-houfe, otherwife then according to this proportion following, (*viz.*) euery Mafter-Printer that is, or hath beene Mafter or vpper Warden of his Company, may haue three Apprentices at one time and no more, and euery Mafter-printer that is of the Liuerie of his Company, may have two Apprentices at one time and no more, and euery Master-printer of the Yeomanry of the Company may haue one Apprentice at one time and no more, neither by Copartnerſhip, binding at the Scriueners, nor any other way whatſoeuer; neither ſhall it be lawfull for any Maſter-Printer when any Apprentice or Apprentices, ſhall run or be put away, to take another Apprentice, or other Apprentices in his or their place or places, vnleſſe the name or names of him or them ſo gone away, be raced out of the Hall-booke, and never admitted again, vpon paine of being for euer diſabled of the vſe of a Preſſe or printing-houſe, and of ſuch further puniſhment, as by this Court or the high Commiſsion Court reſpectiuely, as the ſeuerall cauſes ſhall require, ſhall be thought fit to be impoſed.

XX. *Item*, The Court doth likewiſe declare, that becauſe a great part of the ſecret printing in corners hath been cauſed for want of orderly imployment for Iourneymen printers, Therefore the Court doth hereby require the Maſter and Wardens of the Company of Stationers, to take eſpeciall care that all Iourneymen printers, who are free of the Company of Stationers, ſhall be ſet to worke, and imployed within their owne Company of Stationers; for which purpoſe the Court doth alſo order and declare, that if any Iourneyman Printer, and free of the Company of Stationers, who is of honeſt, and good behauiour, and able in his trade do want imployment, he ſhall repaire to the Maſter and Wardens of the Companie of Stationers, and they or one of them, taking with him or them one or two of the Maſter Printers, ſhall go along with the ſaid Iourneyman-Printer, and ſhall offer his ſeruice in the firſt place to the Maſter Printer vnder whom he ſerued his Apprentiſhip, if he be liuing, and do continue an allowed Printer, or otherwiſe to any other Maſter Printer, whom the Maſter and Wardens of the ſaid Company ſhall thinke fit. And euery Maſter Printer ſhall bee bound to imploy one Iourneyman, being ſo offered to him, and more, if need ſhall ſo require and it fhall be fo adiudged to come to his fhare, according to the proportion of his Apprentices and imployments, by the Mafter and Wardens of the Company of Stationers, although he the faid Mafter Printer with his Apprentice or Apprentices be able without the helpe of the faid Iourneyman or Iourneymen to difcharge his owne worke, vpon paine of fuch punifhment, as by this Court, or the high Commifsion Court refpectiuely, as the feuerall caufes fhall require, fhall be thought fit.

XXI. *Item*, The Court doth declare, That if the Mafter and Wardens of the Companie of Stationers, or any of them, fhall refufe or neglect to go along with any honeft and fufficient Iourney-man Printer, fo defiring their afsiftance, to finde him imployment, vpon complaint and proofe made thereof, he, or they fo offending, fhall fuffer imprifonment, and fuch other punifhment, as by this court, or the high Commifsion Court refpectiuely, as the feuerall caufes fhall require, fhall be thought fit to be impofed. But in cafe any Mafter Printer hath more imployment then he is able to difcharge with helpe of his Apprentice or Apprentices, it fhall be lawful for him to require the helpe of any Iourney-man or Iourney-men-Printers, who are not imployed, and if the faid Iourneyman, or Iourneymen-Printers so required, fhall refufe imployment, or neglect it when hee or they haue vndertaken it, he, or they fhall fuffer imprifonment, and vndergo fuch punifhment, as this Court fhall thinke fit.

XXII. *Item*, The Court doth hereby declare, that it doth not hereby reftraine the Printers of either of the Vniuerfities from taking what number of Apprentices for their feruice in printing there, they themfelues fhall thinke fit. Prouided alwayes, that the faid Printers in the Vniuerfities fhall imploy all their owne Iourney-men within themfelues, and not fuffer any of their faid Iourney-men to go abroad for imployment to the Printers of *London* (vnleffe vpon occafion fome Printers of *London* defire to imploy fome extraordinary Workman or Workmen amongft them, without pre-

iudice to their owne Iourneymen, who are Freemen)
vpon fuch penalty as the Chancellor of either of the
Vniuerfities for the time being, fhall thinke fit to inflict
vpon the delinquents herein.

XXIII. *Item*, That no Mafter-printer fhall imploy
either to worke at the Cafe, or the Preffe, or otherwife
about his printing, any other perfon or perfons, then
fuch onely as are Free-men, or Apprentices to the
Trade or myftery of Printing, vnder paine of being.
difabled for euer after to keep or vfe any Preffe
or Printing-houfe, and fuch further punifhment as by
this Court, or the high Commifsion Court refpectiuely,
as the feuerall caufes fhall require, fhall bee thought
fit to be impofed.

XXIV. *Item*, The Court doth hereby declare their
firme refolution, that if any perfon or perfons, that is
not allowed Printer, fhall hereafter prefume to fet vp
any Preffe for printing, or fhall worke at any fuch
Preffe, or Set, or Compofe any Letters to bee wrought
by any fuch Preffe; hee, or they fo offending, fhall from
time to time, by the Order of this Court, bee fet in the
Pillorie, and Whipt through the Citie of *London*, and
fuffer fuch other punifhment, as this Court fhall Order
or thinke fit to inflict vpon them, vpon Complaint or
proofe of fuch offence or offences, or fhalbe otherwife
punifhed, as the Court of High Commifsion fhall thinke
fit, and is agreeable to their Commifsion.

XXV. *Item*, That for the better difcouery of printing
in Corners without licence ; The Mafter and Wardens
of the Company of Stationers for the time being,
or any two licenfed Mafter-Printers, which fhall be
appointed by the Lord Arch-Bifhop of *Canterbury*, or
Lord B. of *London* for the time being, fhall haue
power and authority, to take vnto themfelues fuch
affiftance as they fhall think needfull, and to fearch
what houfes and fhops (and àt what time they fhall
think fit) efpecially Printing-houfes, and to view what
is in printing, and to call for the licenfe to fee
whether it be licenced or no, and if not, to feize vpon

fo much as is printed, together with the feuerall offenders, and to bring them before the Lord Arch-Bifhop of *Canterbury*, or the Lord Bifhop of *London* for the time being, that they or either of them may take fuch further order therein as fhall appertaine to Iuftice.

XXVI. *Item*, The Court doth declare, that it fhall be lawfull alfo for the faid Searchers, if vpon fearch they find any book or bookes, or part of booke or books which they fufpect to containe matter in it or them, contrary to the doctrine and difcipline of the Church of *England*, or againft the State and Gouernment, vpon fuch fufpition to feize upon fuch book or books, or part of booke or books, and to bring it, or them, to the Lord Arch-Bifhop of *Canterbury*, or the Lord Bifhop of *London* for the time being, who fhall take fuch further courfe therein, as to their Lordfhips, or either of them fhall feeme fit.

XXVII. *Item*, The Court doth order and declare, that there fhall be foure Founders of letters for printing allowed, and no more, and doth hereby nominate, allow, and admit thefe perfons, whofe names hereafter follow, to the number of foure, to be letter-Founders for the time being, (viz) *John Grismand, Thomas Wright, Arthur Nichols, Alexander Fifeild*. And further, the Court doth Order and Decree, that it fhall be lawfull for the Lord Arch-bifhop of *Canterbury*, or the Lord Bifhop of *London* for the time being, taking unto him or them, fix other high Commifsioners, to fupply the place or places of thefe who are now allowed Founders of letters by this Court, as they fhall fall void by death, cenfure, or otherwife.

Prouided, that they exceede not the number of foure, fet downe by this Court. And if any perfon or perfons, not being an allowed Founder, fhall notwithftanding take vpon him, or them, to Found, or caft letters for printing, vpon complaint and proofe made of fuch offence, or offences, he, or they fo offending, fhal fuffer fuch punifhment, as this Court, or the high Commifsion court respectiuely, as the feuerall

caufes fhall require, fhall think fit to inflict vpon
them.

XXVIII. *Item*, That no Mafter-Founder whatfoeuer
fhall keepe aboue two Apprentices at one time, neither
by Copartnerfhip, binding at the Scriueners, nor any
other way whatfoeuer, neither fhall it be lawfull for any
Mafter-Founder, when any Apprentice, or Apprentices
fhall run, or be put away, to take another Apprentice,
or other Apprentices in his, or their place or places,
vnleffe the name or names of him, or them fo gone
away, be rafed out of the Hall-booke of the Company,
where of the Mafter-Founder is free, and never admitted
again, vpon pain of fuch punifhment, as by this Court,
or the high Commifsion refpectiuely, as the feuerall
caufes fhall require, fhall be thought fit to bee impofed.

XXIX. *Item*, That all Iourney-men-Founders be
imployed by the Mafter-Founders of the faid trade,
and that idle Iourney-men be compelled to worke after
the fame manner, and vpon the fame penalties, as in
cafe of the Iourney-men-Printers is before specified.

XXX. *Item*, That no Mafter-Founder of letters,
fhall imploy any other perfon or perfons in any worke
belonging to the cafting or founding of letters, then
fuch only as are freemen or apprentices to the trade of
founding letters, faue onely in the pulling off the knots
of mettle hanging at the ends of the letters when they
are firft caft, in which work it fhall be lawfull for
euery Mafter-Founder, to imploy one boy only that is
not, nor hath beene bound to the trade of Founding
letters, but not otherwife, upon pain of being for euer
difabled to vfe or exercife that art, and fuch further
punifhment, as by this Court, or the high Commifsion
Court refpectiuely, as the feuerall caufes fhall require,
be thought fit to be impofed.

XXXI. *Item*, That euery perfon or perfons whatfoeuer, which fhall at any time or times hereafter, by his
or their confefsion, or otherwife by proof be conuicted
of any of the offences, by this, or any other Decree of
this Court made, fhal before fuch time as he or they

fhall be difcharged, and ouer and aboue their fine and punifhment, as aforefaid, be bound with good fureties, never after to tranfgreffe, or offend in that or the like kinde, for which he, or they fhalbe fo conuicted and punifhed, as aforefaid; And that all and euery the forfeitures aforefaid (excepting all feditious fchifmaticall Bookes, or Pamphlets, which this Court doth hereby Order to bee presently burnt) And except fuch Bookes, as the forfeitures are already granted by Letters Patents, fhall be diuided and difpofed of, as the high Commifsion Court fhall find fit. Alwaies prouiding that one moitie be to the King.

XXXII. *Item*, That no Merchant, Mafter, or Owner of any Ship or Veffell, or any other perfon or perfons whatfoeuer fhall hereafter prefume to land, or put on fhore any Booke or Bookes, or the part of any Booke or Books, to be imported from beyond the feas, in any Port, Hauen, Creek, or other place whatfoeuer within the Realme of *England*, but only in the Port of the City of *London*, to the end the faid Bookes may there be viewed, as aforefaid : And the feuerall Officers of His Maiefties Ports are hereby required to take notice thereof.

XXXIII. *Item*, That whereas there is an agreement betwixt Sir *Thomas Bodley* Knight, Founder of the Vniuerfity Library at *Oxford*, and the Mafter, Wardens, and Afsiftants of the Company of Stationers (*viz.*) That one Booke of euery fort that is new printed, or reprinted with additions, be fent to the Vniuerfitie of *Oxford* for the vfe of the publique Librarie there ; The Court doth hereby Order, and declare, That euery Printer fhall referue one Book new printed, or reprinted by him, with additions, and fhall before any publique venting of the faid book, bring it to the Common Hall of the Companie of Stationers, and deliuer it to the Officer thereof to be fent to the Librarie at *Oxford* accordingly, vpon paine of imprifonment, and fuch further Order and Direction therein, as to this Court, or the high Commifsion Court refpectiuely, as the feuerall caufes fhall require, fhall be thought fit.

FINIS.

An Order made by the Honourable Houſe of Commons.
Die Sabbati, 29, *Janu..rii.* 1641 [1642].

I T is ordered that the Maſter and Wardens of the Company of Stationers ſhall be required to take eſpeciall Order, that the Printers doe neither print, nor reprint any thing without the name and conſent of the Author: And that if any Printer ſhall notwithſtanding print or reprint any thing without the conſent and name of the Author, that he ſhall then be proceeded againſt, as both Printer and Author thereof, and their names to be certified to this Houſe. *H. Elſinge Cler. Parl. do. Com.*

Die Iovis 9. Martii 1642 [1643].
An Order of the Commons aſſembled in Parliament For regulating Printing.

I T is this day Ordered by the Commons Houſe of Parliament, That the Committee for Examinations, or any foure of them, have power to appoint ſuch perſons as they thinke fit, to ſearch in any houſe or place where there is iuſt cauſe of ſuſpition, That Preſſes are kept and employed in the printing of ſcandalous and lying Pamphlets, and that they do demolliſh and take away ſuch Preſſes and their materials, and the Printers Nuts and Spindles which they find ſo employed, and bring the Maſter-Printers, and Workmen Printers before the ſaid Committee ; and that the Committee or any four of them, have power to commit to priſon any of the ſaid Printers, or any other perſons that do contrive, or publikely or privately vend ſell, or publiſh any Pamphlet ſcandalous to his Majeſty or the proceedings of both or either Houſes of Parliament, or that ſhall refuſe to ſuffer any Houſes or Shops to be ſearched, where ſuch preſſes or pamphlets as aforeſaid are kept : And that the perſons imployed by the ſaid Committee ſhall have power to ſeize ſuch ſcandalous and lying pamphlets as they find uppon ſearch, to be in any ſhopp or warhouſe, ſold, or diſperſed by any perſon whomſoever, and to bring the perſons (that ſo kept publiſhed, or ſold the ſame,) before the Committee ; And that ſuch perſons as the Committee ſhall commit for any offences aforeſaid, ſhall not be releaſed till the parties imployed for the apprehending of the ſaid perſons, and ſeizing their preſſes and materialls, be ſatisfied for their paines and charges. And all Iuſtices of the Peace, Captains, Officers, and Conſtables, are required to be aſiſting in the apprehending of any the perſons aforeſaid, And in ſearching of their ſhopps, Houſes, and Warehouſes ; And likewiſe all Iuſtices of peace, Officers, and Conſtables, are hereby required from time to time to apprehend ſuch perſons as ſhall publiſh, vend, or ſell the ſaid pamphlets. And it is further ordered, That this Order be forthwith printed and publiſhed, to the end that notice may be taken thereof, that the contemners of this Order may be left inexcuſable for their offence. [*A Collection of all the publicke Orders Ordinances and Declarations, &c.* by EDWARD HUSBAND, p 1. London. 1646.

AN

ORDER

OF THE

LORDS and COMMONS

Affembled in Parliament.

For the

Regulating of Printing,

And

For fuppreffing the great late abufes
and frequent diforders in Printing many falfe,
Scandalous, Seditious, Libellous, and unlicenfed
Pamphlets, to the great defamation of
Religion and Government.

Also, authorizing the Mafters & Wardens of
the Company of *Stationers* to make diligent fearch, feize
and carry away all fuch Books as they fhall finde Printed, or
reprinted by any man having no lawfull intereft in
them, being entred into the Hall Book to
any other man as his proper Copies.

Die Mercurii. 14 June. 1643.

ORdered by the Lords and Commons affembled in Parliament,
that this Order fhall be forthwith printed and published.

J. Brown Cler. Parliamentorum:
Hen. Elsing Cler. D. Com.

LONDON, Printed for *I. Wright* in the Old-baily, *Iune* 16, 1643.

Die Mercurii, 14 *Junii.* 1643.

HEREAS divers good Orders have bin lately made by both Houfes of Parliament, for fuppreffing the great late abufes and frequent diforders in Printing many, falfe forged, fcandalous, feditious, libellous, and unlicenfed Papers, Pamphlets, and Books to the great defamation of Religion and government. Which orders (notwithftanding the diligence of the Company of *Stationers,* to put them in full execution) have taken little or no effect : By reafon the bill in preparation, for redreffe of the faid diforders, hath hitherto bin retarded through the prefent diftractions, and very many, aswell *Stationers* and *Printers,* as others of fundry other profeffions not free of the *Stationers* Company, have taken upon them to fet up fundry private Printing Preffes in corners, and to print, vend, publifh and difperfe Books, pamphlets and papers, in fuch multitudes, that no induftry could be fufficient to difcover or bring to punifhment, all the feverall abounding delinquents ; And by reafon that divers of the *Stationers* Company and others being Delinquents (contrary to former orders and the conftant cuftome ufed among the faid Company) have taken liberty to Print, Vend and publifh, the moft profitable vendible Copies of Books, belonging to the Company and other *Stationers,* efpecially of fuch Agents as are imployed in putting the faid Orders in Execution, and that by way of revenge for giveing information againft them to the Houfes for their Delinquences in Printing, to the great prejudice of the faid Company of *Stationers* and Agents, and to their difcouragement in this publik fervice.

It is therefore Ordered by the Lords and Commons in *Parliament,* That no Order or Declaration of both, or either Houfe of *Parliament* fhall be printed by any, but by order of one or both the faid Houfes : Nor other Book, Pamphlet, paper, nor part of any fuch Book, Pamphlet, or paper, fhall from henceforth be printed, bound, ftitched or put to fale by any perfon or perfons whatfoever, unleffe the fame be firft approved of and licenfed under the hands of fuch perfon or perfons as both, or either of the faid Houfes fhall appoint for the licenfing of the fame, and entred in the Regifter Book of the Company of *Stationers*, according to Ancient cuftom, and the Printer thereof to put his name thereto. And that no perfon or perfons fhall hereafter print, or caufe to be reprinted any Book or Books, or part of Book, or Books heretofore allowed of and granted to the faid Company of *Stationers* for their relief and maintenance of their poore, without the licence or confent of the Mafter, Wardens and Affiftants of the faid Company; Nor any Book or Books lawfully licenced and entred in the Regifter of the faid Company for any particular member thereof, without the licence and confent of the owner or owners thereof. Nor yet import any such Book or Books, or part of Book or Books formerly Printed here, from beyond the Seas, upon paine of forfeiting the fame to the Owner, or Owners of the Copies of the faid Books, and fuch further punifhment as fhall be thought fit.

And the Master and Wardens of the faid Company, the Gentleman Ufher of the Houfe of *Peers*, the Sergeant of the Commons Houfe and their deputies, together with the perfons formerly appointed by the Committee of the Houfe of Commons for Examinations, are hereby Authorized and required, from time to time, to make diligent fearch in all places, where they fhall think meete, for all unlicenfed Printing Preffes, and all Preffes any way imployed in the printing of fcandalous or unlicenfed Papers, Pamphlets, Books, or any Copies of Books belonging to the faid Company, or any member thereof, without their approbation and confents, and to feize and carry away fuch Printing Preffes Letters, together with the Nut, Spindle,

and other materialls of every fuch irregular Printer,
which they find fo mifimployed, unto the Common
Hall of the faid Company, there to be defaced and
made unferviceable according to Ancient Cuftom ;
And likewife to make diligent fearch in all fufpected
Printing-houfes, Ware-houfes, Shops and other places
for fuch fcandalous and unlicenfed Books, papers,
Pamphlets, and all other Books, not entred, nor figned
with the Printers name as aforefaid, being printed, or
reprinted by fuch as have no lawfull intereft in them,
or any way contrary to this Order, and the fame to
seize and carry away to the faid common hall, there to
remain till both or either Houfe of *Parliament* fhall
difpofe thereof, And likewife to apprehend all Authors,
Printers, and other perfons whatfoever imployed in
compiling, printing, ftitching, binding, publifhing and
difperfing of the faid fcandalous, unlicenfed, and un-
warrantable papers, books and pamphlets as aforefaid,
and all thofe who fhall refift the faid Parties in fearching after them, and to bring them afore either of the
Houfes or the Committee of Examinations, that fo they
may receive fuch further punifhments, as their Offences
fhall demerit, and not to be releafed untill they have
given fatisfaction to the Parties imployed in their apprehenfion for their paines and charges, and given
sufficient caution not to offend in like fort for the
future.   And all Juftices of the Peace, Captaines, Con-
ftables and other officers, are hereby ordered and
required to be aiding, and affifting to the forefaid perfons in the due execution of all, and fingular the prem-
iffes and in the apprehenfion of all Offenders againft
the fame.   And in cafe of oppofition to break open
Doores and Locks.

   And it is further ordered, that this Order be forthwith Printed and Publifhed, to the end that notice
may be taken thereof, and all Contemners of it left
inexcufable.

FINIS.

AREOPAGITICA;

A

SPEECH

OF

Mr· *JOHN MILTON*

For the Liberty of Vnlicenc'd

PRINTING,

To the Parlament of ENGLAND.

Τὸλέυθερον δ'ἐκεῖνο, ἔι τις θέλει πόλει
Χρησόν τι βύλευμ' εἰς μέσον φέρειν, ἔχων.
Καὶ ταῦθ' ὁ χρῄζων, λαμπρὸς ἔσθ', ὁ μὴ θέλων,
Σιγᾷ, τί τẃτων ἐσιν ἰσαίτερον πόλει;

                    Euripid. Hicetid.

This is true Liberty when free born men
Having to advise the public may speak free,
Which he who can, and will, deserv's high praise,
Who neither can nor will, may hold his peace;
What can be juster in a State then this?

                    Euripid. Hicetid.

LONDON,
Printed in the Yeare, 1644.

For the Liberty of unlicenc'd Printing.

THey who to States and Governours of the Commonwealth direct their Speech, High Court of Parlament, or wanting fuch acceffe in a private condition, write that which they forefee may advance the publick good ; I fuppofe them as at the beginning of no meane endeavour, not a little alter'd and mov'd inwardly in their mindes : Some with doubt of what will be the fucceffe, others with feare of what will be the cenfure ; fome with hope, others with confidence of what they have to fpeake. And me perhaps each of thefe difpofitions, as the fub- ject was whereon I enter'd, may have at other times varioufly affected ; and likely might in thefe foremoft expreffions now alfo difclofe which of them fway'd moft, but that the very attempt of this addreffe thus made, and the thought of whom it hath recourfe to, hath got the power within me to a paffion, farre more welcome then incidentall to a Preface. Which though I ftay not to confeffe ere any afke, I fhall be blameleffe, if it be no other, then the joy and gratulation which it brings to all who wifh and promote their Countries liberty ; whereof this whole Difcourfe propof'd will be a certaine teftimony, if not a Trophey. For this is not the liberty which wee can hope, that no grievance ever fhould arife in the Commonwealth, that let no man in this World expect ; but when complaints are freely heard, deeply confider'd, and fpeedily reform'd, then is the utmoft bound of civill liberty attain'd that wife men

looke for. To which if I now manifeſt by the very ſound
of this which I ſhall utter, that wee are already in good
part arriv'd, and yet from ſuch a ſteepe diſadvantage of
tyranny and ſuperſtition grounded into our principles
as was beyond the manhood of a *Roman* recovery, it
will bee attributed firſt, as is moſt due, to the ſtrong
aſſiſtance of God our deliverer, next to your faithfull
guidance and undaunted Wiſdome, Lords and Commons
of *England*. Neither is it in Gods eſteeme the diminu-
tion of his glory, when honourable things are ſpoken of
good men and worthy Magiſtrates ; which if I now firſt
ſhould begin to doe, after ſo fair a progreſſe of your
laudable deeds, and ſuch a long obligement upon the
whole Realme to your indefatigable vertues, I might
be juſtly reckn'd among the tardieſt, and the unwilling-
eſt of them that praiſe yee. Neverthelefſe there being
three principall things, without which all praiſing is but
Courtſhip and flattery, Firſt, when that only is prais'd
which is ſolidly worth praiſe : next, when greateſt like-
lihoods are brought that ſuch things are truly and really
in thoſe perſons to whom they are aſcrib'd, the other,
when he who praiſes, by ſhewing that ſuch his actuall
perſwaſion is of whom he writes, can demonſtrate that
he flatters not ; the former two of theſe I have heretofore endeavour'd, reſcuing the employment from him
who went about to impaire your merits with a triviall and
malignant *Encomium ;* the latter as belonging chiefly to
mine owne acquittall, that whom I ſo extoll'd I did not
flatter, hath been reſerv'd opportunely to this occaſion.
For he who freely magnifies what hath been nobly done,
and fears not to declare as freely what might be done
better, gives ye the beſt cov'nant of his fidelity ; and
that his loyaleſt affection and his hope waits on your
proceedings. His higheſt praiſing is not flattery, and
his plaineſt advice is a kinde of praiſing ; for though I
ſhould affirme and hold by argument, that it would fare
better with truth, with learning, and the Commonwealth,
if one of your publiſht Orders which I ſhould name, were
call'd in, yet at the ſame time it could not but much

redound to the luftre of your milde and equall Government, when as private perfons are hereby animated to
thinke ye better pleas'd with publick advice, then other
ftatifts have been delighted heretofore with publicke
flattery. And men will then fee what difference there
is between the magnanimity of a trienniall Parlament,
and that jealous hautineffe of Prelates and cabin Coun-
fellours that ufurpt of late, when as they fhall obferve
yee in the midd'ft of your Victories and fucceffes more
gently brooking writt'n exceptions againft a voted Order,
then other Courts, which had produc't nothing worth
memory but the weake oftentation of wealth, would have
endur'd the leaft fignifi'd diflike at any fudden Procla-
mation. If I fhould thus farre prefume upon the meek
demeanour of your civill and gentle greatneffe, Lords
and Commons, as wnat your publifht Order hath directly
faid, that to gainfay, I might defend my felfe with eafe,
if any fhould accufe me of being new or infolent, did
they but know how much better I find ye efteem it to
imitate the old and elegant humanity of Greece, then
the barbarick pride of a *Hunnifh* and *Norwegian* ftate-
lines. And out of thofe ages, to whofe polite wifdom
and letters we ow that we are not yet *Gothes* and *Jut-
landers*, I could name him who from his private houfe
wrote that difcourfe to the Parlament of *Athens*, that
perfwades them to change the forme of *Democraty* which
was then eftablifht. Such honour was done in thofe
dayes to men who profeft the ftudy of wifdome and elo-
quence, not only in their own Country, but in other
Lands, that Cities and Siniories heard them gladly, and
with great refpect, if they had ought in publick to admonifh the State. Thus did *Dion Prufæus* a ftranger
and a privat Orator counfell the *Rhodians* againft a
former Edict : and I abound with other like examples,
which to fet heer would be fuperfluous. But if from
the induftry of a life wholly dedicated to ftudious labours,
and thofe naturall endowments haply not the worft for
two and fifty degrees of northern latitude, fo much muft
be derogated, as to count me not equall to any of thofe

who had this priviledge, I would obtain to be thought not fo inferior, as your felves are fuperior to the moft of them who receiv'd their counfell : and how farre you excell them, be affur'd, Lords and Commons, there can no greater teftimony appear, then when your prudent fpirit acknowledges and obeyes the voice of reafon from what quarter foever it be heard fpeaking ; and renders ye as willing to repeal any Act of your own fetting forth, as any fet forth by your Predeceffors.

If ye be thus refolv'd, as it were injury to thinke ye were not, I know not what fhould withhold me from prefenting ye with a fit inftance wherein to fhew both that love of truth which ye eminently profeffe, and that uprightneffe of your judgement which is not wont to be partiall to your felves ; by judging over again that Order which ye have ordain'd *to regulate Printing.*[3]   *That no Book, pamphlet, or paper fhall be henceforth Printed, un-leffe the fame be firft approv'd and licenc't by fuch,* or at leaft one of fuch as fhall be thereto appointed.   For that part which preferves juftly every mans Copy to himfelfe, or provides for the poor, I touch not, only wifh they be not made pretenfes to abufe and perfecute honeft and painfull Men, who offend not in either of thefe particulars.   But that other claufe of Licencing Books, which we thought had dy'd with his brother *quadragefimal* and *matrimonial* when the Prelats expir'd, I fhall now attend with fuch a Homily, as fhall lay before ye, firft the inventors of it to bee thofe whom ye will be loath to own ; next what is to be thought in generall of reading, what ever fort the Books be ; and that this Order avails nothing to the fuppreffing of fcandalous, feditious, and libellous Books, which were mainly intended to be fupp-reft.   Laft, that it will be primely to the difcourage-ment of all learning, and the ftop of Truth, not only by the difexercifing and blunting our abilities in what we know already, but by hindring and cropping the dif-covery that might bee yet further made both in religious and civill Wifdome.

I deny not, but that it is of greateft concernment in

the Church and Commonwealth, to have a vigilant eye how Bookes demeane themfelves as well as men ; and thereafter to confine, imprifon, and do fharpeſt juſtice on them as malefactors : For Books are not abfolutely dead things, but doe contain a potencie of life in them to be as active as that foule was whofe progeny they are ; nay they do preferve as in a violl the pureſt efficacie and extraction of that living intellect that bred them. I know they are as lively, and as vigoroufly productive, as thofe fabulous Dragons teeth ; and being fown up and down, may chance to fpring up armed men. And yet on the other hand unleffe warineffe be us'd, as good almoſt kill a Man as kill a good Book ; who kills a Man kills a reafonable creature, Gods Image ; but hee who deſtroyes a good Booke, kills reafon it felfe, kills the Image of God, as it were in the eye. Many a man lives a burden to the Earth ; but a good Booke is the pretious life-blood of a maſter fpirit, imbalm'd and treafur'd up on purpofe to a life beyond life. 'Tis true, no age can reſtore a life, whereof perhaps there is no great loffe ; and revolutions of ages doe not oft recover the loffe of a rejected truth, for the want of which whole Nations fare the worfe. We fhould be wary therefore what perfecution we raife againſt the living labours of publick men, how we fpill that feafon'd life of man preferv'd and ſtor'd up in Books ; fince we fee a kinde of homicide may be thus committed, fometimes a martyrdome, and if it extend to the whole impreffion, a kinde of maffacre, whereof the execution ends not in the flaying of an elementall life, but ſtrikes at that ethereall and fift effence, the breath of reafon it felfe, flaies an immortality rather then a life. But leſt I fhould be condemn'd of introducing licence, while I oppofe Licencing, I refufe not the paines to be fo much Hiſtoricall, as will ferve to fhew what hath been done by ancient and famous Commonwealths, againſt this diforder, till the very time that this project of licencing crept out of the *Inquifition,* was catcht up by our Prelates, and hath caught fome of our Prefbyters.

In *Athens* where Books and Wits were ever bufier then in any other part of *Greece*, I find but only two sorts of writings which the Magiſtrate car'd to take notice of; thoſe either blaſphemous and Atheiſticall, or Libellous. Thus the Books of *Protagoras* were by the Judges of *Areopagus* commanded to be burnt, and himſelfe baniſht the territory for a diſcourſe begun with his confeſſing not to know *whether there were gods, or whether not :* And againſt defaming, it was decreed that none ſhould be traduc'd by name, as was the manner of *Vetus Comœdia*, whereby we may gueſſe how they cenſur'd libelling : And this courſe was quick enough, as *Cicero* writes, to quell both the deſperate wits of other Atheiſts, and the open way of defaming, as the event ſhew'd. Of other ſects and opinions though tending to voluptuouſneſſe, and the denying of divine providence they tooke no heed. Therefore we do not read that either *Epicurus*, or that libertine ſchool of *Cyrene*, or what the *Cynick* impudence utter'd, was ever queſtion'd by the Laws. Neither is it recorded that the writings of thoſe old Comedians were ſuppreſt, though the acting of them were forbid ; and that *Plato* commended the reading of *Ariſtophanes* the looſeſt of them all, to his royall ſcholler *Dionyſius*, is commonly known, and may be excus'd, if holy *Chryſoſtome*, as is reported, nightly ſtudied ſo much the ſame Author and had the art to cleanſe a ſcurrilous vehemence into the ſtill of a rouſing Sermon. That other leading City of *Greece*, *Lacedæmon*, conſidering that *Lycurgus* their Law-giver was ſo addicted to elegant learning, as to have been the firſt that brought out of *Ionia* the ſcatter'd workes of *Homer*, and ſent the Poet *Thales* from *Creet* to prepare and mollifie the *Spartan* ſurlineſſe with his ſmooth ſongs and odes, the better to plant among them law and civility, it is to be wonder'd how muſeieſs and unbookiſh they were, minding nought but the feats of Warre. There needed no licencing of Books among them for they diſlik'd all, but their owne *Laconick Apothegms*, and took a ſlight occaſion to chaſe *Archilochus*

out of their City, perhaps for compoſing in a higher
ſtraine then their owne ſouldierly ballats and roundels
could reach to : Or if it were for his broad verſes, they
were not therein ſo cautious, but they were as diſſolute
in their promiſcuous converſing; whence *Euripides*
affirmes in *Andromache,* that their women were all un-
chaſte. Thus much may give us light after what ſort
Bookes were prohibited among the Greeks. The Ro-
mans alſo for many ages train'd up only to a military
roughnes, reſembling moſt of the *Lacedæmonian* guiſe,
knew of learning little but what their twelve Tables,
and the *Pontifick* College with their *Augurs* and *Flamins*
taught them in Religion and Law, ſo unacquainted with
other learning, that when *Carneades* and *Critolaus,* with
the *Stoick Diogenes* comming Embaſſadors to Rome,
tooke thereby occaſion to give the City a taſt of their
Philoſophy, they were ſuſpected for ſeducers by no leſſe
a man then *Cato* the Cenſor, who mov'd it in the Senat
to diſmiſſe them ſpeedily, and to baniſh all ſuch *Attick*
bablers out of *Italy.* But *Scipio* and others of the
nobleſt Senators withſtood him and his old *Sabin* auſ-
terity ; honour'd and admir'd the men ; and the Cenſor
himſelf at laſt in his old age fell to the ſtudy of that
whereof before hee was ſo ſcrupulous. And yet at the
ſame time *Nævius* and *Plautus* the firſt Latine comedians had fill'd the City with all the borrow'd Scenes of
Menander and *Philemon.* Then began to be conſider'd
there alſo what was to be don to libellous books and
Authors ; for *Nævius* was quickly caſt into priſon for
his unbridl'd pen, and releas'd by the *Tribunes* upon his
recantation : We read alſo that libels were burnt, and
the makers puniſht by *Auguſtus.* The like ſeverity no
doubt was us'd if ought were impiouſly writt'n againſt
their eſteemed gods. Except in theſe two points, how
the world went in Books, the Magiſtrat kept no reck-
ning. And therefore *Lucretius* without impeachment
verſifies his Epicuriſm to *Memmius,* and had the honour
to be ſetforth the ſecond time by *Cicero* ſo great a father
of the Commonwealth ; although himſelfe diſputes

againſt that opinion in his own writings.   Nor was the
Satyricall ſharpneſſe, or naked plainnes of *Lucilius*, or
Catullus, or *Flaccus*, by any order prohibited.   And for
matters of State, the ſtory of *Titius Livius*, though it
extoll'd that part which *Pompey* held, was not therefore
ſuppreſt by *Octavius Cæsar* of the other Faction.   But
that *Naſo* was by him baniſht in his old age, for the
wanton Poems of his youth, was but a meer covert of
State over ſome ſecret cauſe : and beſides, the Books
were neither baniſht nor call'd in.   From hence we ſhall
meet with little elſe but tyranny in the Roman Empire,
that we may not marvell, if not ſo often bad, as good
Books were ſilenc't.   I ſhall therefore deem to have
bin large anough in producing what among the ancients
was puniſhable to write, ſave only which, all other arguments were free to treat on.

   By this time the Emperours were become Chriſtians,
whoſe diſcipline in this point I doe not finde to have
bin more ſevere then what was formerly in practice.
The Books of thoſe whom they took to be grand Hereticks were examin'd, refuted, and condemn'd in the
generall Councels ; and not till then were prohibited,
or burnt by autority of the Emperor.   As for the
writings of Heathen authors, unleſſe they were plaine
invectives againſt Chriſtianity, as thoſe of *Porphyrius*
and *Proclus*, they met with no interdict that can be
cited, till about the year 400, in a *Carthaginian* Councel,
wherein Biſhops themſelves were forbid to read the
Books of Gentiles, but Hereſies they might read : while
others long before them on the contrary ſcrupl'd more
the Books of Hereticks, then of Gentiles.   And that
the primitive Councels and Biſhops were wont only to
declare what Books were not commendable, paſſing no
furder, but leaving it to each ones conſcience to read
or to lay by, till after the year 800 is obſerv'd already by
Padre Paolo the great unmaſker of the *Trentine* Councel.
After which time the Popes of *Rome* engroſſing what
they pleas'd of Politicall rule into their owne hands,
extended their dominion over mens eyes, as they had

before over their judgements, burning and prohibiting
to be read, what they fanfied not ; yet fparing in their
cenfures, and the Books not many which they fo dealt
with : till *Martin* the 5. by his Bull not only prohibited,
but was the firft that excommunicated the reading of
hereticall Books ; for about. that time *Wicklef* and
Huffe growing terrible, were they who firft drove the
Papall Court to a ftricter policy of prohibiting. Which
cours *Leo* the 10, and his fucceffors follow'd, untill the
Councell of Trent, and the Spanifh Inquifition engen-
dring together brought forth, or perfeted thofe Cata-
logues, and expurging Indexes that rake through the
entralls of many an old good Author, with a violation
wors then any could be offer'd to his tomb. Nor did
they ftay in matters Hereticall, but any fubject that was
not to their palat, they either condemn'd in a prohibition, or had it ftrait into the new Purgatory of an Index.
To fill up the meafure of encroachment, their laft invention was to ordain that no Book, pamphlet, or paper
fhould be Printed (as if *S. Peter* had bequeath'd them
the keys of the Preffe alfo out of Paradife) unleffe it
were approv'd and licenc't under the hands of 2 or 3
glutton Friers. For example :

Let the Chancellor *Cini* be pleas'd to fee if in this
prefent work be contain'd ought that may withftand the
Printing,

Vincent Rabatta Vicar of *Florence.*

I have feen this prefent work, and finde nothing
athwart the Catholick faith and good manners : In
witneffe whereof I have given, &c.

Nicolò Cini, Chancellor of *Florence.*

Attending the precedent relation, it is allow'd that
this prefent work of *Davanzati*⁴ may be Printed,

Vincent Rabatta, &c.

It may be Printed, *July* 15.

Friar *Simon Mompei d'Amelia* Chancellor of
the holy office in *Florence.*

Sure they have a conceit, if he of the bottomleffe

pit had not long fince broke prifon, that this quadruple exorcifm would barre him down. I feare their next defigne will be to get into their cuftody the licencing of that which they fay *Claudius* intended, but went not through with. Voutfafe to fee another of their forms the Roman ftamp :

* Quo veniam daret flatum crepitumque ventris in convivio emitendi. Sueton. in Claudio.

Imprimatur, If it ˊeem good to the reverend Mafter of the holy Palace,

> *Belcastro*, Vicegerent.

Imprimatur,

Friar *Nicolò Rodolphi* Mafter of the holy Palace. Sometimes 5 *Imprimaturs* are feen together dialoguewife in the Piatza of one Title page, complementing and ducking each to other with their shav'n reverences, whether the Author, who ftands by in perplexity at the foot of his Epiftle, fhall to the Preffe or to the fpunge. ·Thefe are the prety refponfories, thefe are the deare Antiphonies that fo bewitcht of late our Prelats, and their Chaplaines with the goodly Eccho they made ; and befotted us to the gay imitation of a lordly *Imprimatur*, one from Lambeth houfe, another from the Weft end of *Pauls ;* fo apifhly Romanizing, that the word of command ftill was fet downe in Latine ; as if the learned Grammaticall pen that wrote it, would caft no ink without Latine ; or perhaps, as they thought, becaufe no vulgar tongue was worthy to expreffe the pure conceit of an *Imprimatur* ; but rather, as I hope, for that our Englifh, the language of men ever famous, and formoft in the achievements of liberty, will not eafily finde fervile letters anow to fpell fuch a dictatorie prefumption Englifh.   And thus ye have the Inventors and the originall of Book-licencing ript up, and drawn as lineally as any pedigree.   We have it not, that can be heard of, from any ancient State, or politie, or Church, nor by any Statute left us by our Anceftors, elder or later ; nor from the moderne cuftom of any reformed Citty, or Church abroad ; but from the moft Antichriftian Councel, and the moft tyrannous Inquifition that ever inquir'd. Till then Books were ever as freely admitted into the World as any other birth; the iffue of the brain was no more ftifl'd then the iffue of the womb: no envious *Juno* sate crofs-leg'd over the nativity of any mans intellectual off spring; but if it prov'd a Monfter, who denies, but that it was juftly burnt, or funk in the Sea. But that a Book in wors condition then a peccant foul, fhould be to ftand before a Jury ere it be borne to the World, and undergo yet in darkneffe the judgement of *Radamanth* and his Colleagues, ere it can paffe the ferry backward into light, was never heard before, till that myfterious iniquity provokt and troubl'd at the firft entrance of Reformation, fought out new limbo's and new hells wherein they might include our Books alfo within the number of their damned. And this was the rare morfell fo officioufly fnatcht up, and fo ilfavourdly imitated by our inquifiturient Bifhops, and the attendant minorites their Chaplains. That ye like not now thefe moft certain Authors of this licencing order, and that all finifter intention was farre diftant from your thoughts, when ye were importun'd the paffing it, all men who know the integrity of your actions, and how ye honour Truth, will clear yee readily.

But fome will fay, what though the Inventors were bad, the thing for all that may be good? It may fo: yet if that thing be no fuch deep invention, but obvious, and eafie for any man to light on, and yet beft and wifeft Commonwealths through all ages, and occafions have forborne to ufe it, and falfeft feducers, and oppreffors of men were the firft who tooke it up, and to no other purpofe but to obftruct and hinder the firft approach of Reformation; I am of thofe who beleeve, it will be a harder alchymy then *Lullius* ever knew, to sublimat any good ufe out of fuch an invention. Yet this only is what I requeft to gain from this reafon, that it may be held a dangerous and fufpicious fruit, as certainly it deferves, for the tree that bore it, untill I can diffect one by one the properties it has. But I have firft to finifh, as was propounded, what is to be

thought in generall of reading Books, what ever fort
they be, and whether be more the benefit, or the harm
that thence proceeds?

Not to infift upon the examples of *Mofes, Daniel*
and *Paul,* who were fkilfull in all the learning of the
Ægyptians, Caldeans, and Greeks, which could not
probably be without reading their Books of all forts, in
Paul efpecially, who thought it no defilement to infert
into holy Scripture the fentences of three Greek Poets,
and one of them a Tragedian, the queftion was,
notwithftanding fometimes controverted among the
Primitive Doctors, but with great odds on that fide
which affirm'd it both lawfull and profitable, as was
then evidently perceiv'd, when *Julian* the Apoftat, and
futtleft enemy to our faith, made a decree forbidding
Chriftians the ftudy of heathen learning : for, faid he,
they wound us with our own weapons, and with our
owne arts and fciences they overcome us. And indeed
the Chriftians were put fo to their fhifts by this crafty
means, and fo much in danger to decline into all ignorance, that the two *Apollinarii* were fain as a man may
fay, to coin all the feven liberall Sciences out of the
Bible, reducing it into divers forms of Orations, Poems,
Dialogues, ev'n to the calculating of a new Chriftian
Grammar. But faith the Hiftorian *Socrates,* The providence of God provided better then the induftry of
Apollinarius and his fon, by taking away that illiterat
law with the life of him who devis'd it. So great an injury they then held it to be depriv'd of *Hellenick* learning ; and thought it a perfecution more undermining,
and fecretly decaying the Church then the open
cruelty of *Decius* or *Dioclefian.* And perhaps it was
the fame politick drift that the Divell whipt St. *Jerom*
in a lenten dream, for reading *Cicero* ; or elfe it was a
fantafm bred by the feaver which had then feis'd him.
For had an Angel bin his difcipliner, unleffe it were
for dwelling too much upon Ciceronifms, and had
chatiz'd the reading, not the vanity, it had bin plainly
partiall ; firft to correct him for grave *Cicero,* and not

for fcurrill *Plautus* whom he confeffes to have bin
reading not long before; next to correct him only,
and let fo many more ancient Fathers wax old in thofe
pleafant and florid ftudies without the lafh of fuch a
tutoring apparition ; infomuch that *Bafil* teaches how
fome good ufe may be made of *Margites* a fportfull
Poem, not now extant, writ by *Homer;* and why not
then of *Morgante* an Italian Romanze much to the
fame purpofe. But if it be agreed we fhall be try'd by
vifions, there is a vifion recorded by *Eufebius* far anci-
enter then this tale of *Jerom* to the nun *Euftochium*,
and befides has nothing of a feavor in it. *Dionyfius
Alexandrinus* was about the year 240, a perfon of great
name in the Church for piety and learning, who had
wont to avail himfelf much againft hereticks by being
converfant in their Books; untill a certain Presbyter
laid it fcrupuloufly to his confcience, how he durft
venture himfelfe among thofe defiling volumes. The
worthy man loath to give offence fell into a new debate with himfelfe what was to be thought; when fud-
denly a vifion fent from God, it is his own Epiftle
that fo averrs it, confirm'd him in thefe words : Read
any books what ever come to thy hands, for thou art
fufficient both to judge aright, and to examine each
matter. To this revelation he affented the fooner, as
he confeffes, becaufe it was anfwerable to that of the
Apoftle to the Theffalonians, Prove all things, hold
faft that which is good. And he might have added
another remarkable faying of the fame Author; To the
pure all things are pure, not only meats and drinks, but
all kinde of knowledge whether of good or evill; the
knowledge cannot defile, nor confequently the books,
if the will and confcience be not defil'd. For books
are as meats and viands are, fome of good, fome of
evill fubftance; and yet God in that unapocryphall
vifion, faid without exception, Rife *Peter*, kill and eat,
leaving the choice to each mans difcretion. Whole-
fome meats to a vitiated ftomack differ little or nothing
from unwholefome; and beft books to a naughty mind

are not unappliable to occafions of evill. Bad meats
will fcarce breed good nourifhment in the healthieft
concoction ; but herein the difference is of bad books,
that they to a difcreet and judicious Reader ferve in
many refpects to difcover, to confute, to forewarn, and
to illuftrate. Whereof what better witnes can ye expect
I fhould produce, then one of your own now fitting in
Parlament, the chief of learned men reputed in this
Land, Mr. *Selden,* whofe volume of naturall and
national laws proves, not only by great autorities
brought together, but by exquifite reafons and theorems
almoft mathematically demonftrative, that all opinions,
yea errors, known, read, and collated, are of main fervice and affiftance toward the fpeedy attainment of
what is trueft. I conceive therefore, that when God
did enlarge the univerfall diet of mans body, faving
ever the rules of temperance, he then alfo, as before,
left arbitrary the dyeting and repafting of our minds;
as wherein every mature man might have to exercife his
owne leading capacity. How great a vertue is temperance, how much of moment through the whole life
of man? yet God committs the managing fo great a
truft, without particular Law or prefcription, wholly to
the demeanour of every grown man. And therefore
when he himfelf tabl'd the Jews from heaven, that
Omer which was every mans daily portion of Manna, is
computed to have bin more then might have well fuffic'd
the heartieft feeder thrice as many meals. For thofe
actions which enter into a man, rather then iffue out
of him, and therefore defile not, God ufes not to cap-
tivat under a perpetuall childhood of prefcription, but
trufts him with the gift of reafon to be his own choofer;
there were but little work left for preaching, if law and
compulfion fhow grow fo faft upon those things which
hertofore were govern'd only by exhortation. *Salomon* informs us that much reading is a wearines to the
flefh ; but neither he, nor other infpir'd author tells us
that fuch, or fuch reading is unlawfull : yet certainly had
God thought good to limit us herein, it had bin much

more expedient to have told us what was unlawfull,
then what was wearifome. As for the burning of thofe
Ephefian books by St. *Pauls* converts, tis reply'd the
books were magick, the Syriack fo renders them. It
was a privat act, a voluntary act, and leaves us to
a voluntary imitation : the men in remorfe burnt thofe
books which were their own ; the Magiftrat by this example is not appointed : thefe men practiz'd the books,
another might perhaps have read them in fome fort ufe-
fully. Good and evill we know in the field of this World
grow up together almoft infeparably ; and the knowledge
of good is fo involv'd and interwoven with the knowledge of evill, and in fo many cunning refemblances
hardly to be difcern'd, that thofe confufed feeds which
were impos'd on *Pfyche* as an inceffant labour to cull
out, and fort afunder, were not more intermixt. It
was from out the rinde of one apple tafted, that the
knowledge of good and evill as two twins cleaving together leapt forth into the World. And perhaps this is
that doom which *Adam* fell into of knowing good and
evill, that is to fay of knowing good by evill. As
therefore the ftate of man now is ; what wifdome can
there be to choofe, what continence to forbeare without the knowledge of evill ? He that can apprehend
and confider vice with all her baits and seeming pleafures, and yet abftain, and yet diftinguifh, and yet pre-
fer that which is truly better, he is the true warfaring
Chriftian. I cannot praife a fugitive and cloifter'd
vertue, unexercis'd and unbreath'd, that never fallies
out and fees her adverfary, but flinks out of the race,
where that immortall garland is to be run for, not
without duft and heat. Affuredly we bring not inno-
cence into the world, we bring impurity much rather :
that which purifies us is triall, and triall is by what is
contrary. That vertue therefore which is but a young-
ling in the contemplation of evill, and knows not the
utmoft that vice promifes to her followers, and rejects
it, is but a blank vertue, not a pure ; her whiteneffe is
but an excrementall whiteneffe ; Which was the reafon

why our fage and ferious Poet *Spencer,* whom I dare
be known to think a better teacher then *Scotus* or
Aquinas, defcribing true temperance under the perfon
of *Guion,* brings him in with his palmer through the
cave of Mammon, and the bowr of earthly bliffe that
he might fee and know, and yet abftain. Since therefore the knowledge and furvay of vice is in this world
fo neceffary to the conftituting of human vertue, and
the fcanning of error to the confirmation of truth, how
can we more fafely, and with leffe danger fcout into
the regions of fin and falfity then by reading all manner of tractats, and hearing all manner of reafon ? And
this is the benefit which may be had of books promif-
cuoufly read. But of the harm that may refult hence
three kinds are ufually reckn'd. Firft, is fear'd the
infection that may fpread ; but then all human learning
and controverfie in religious points must remove out
of the world, yea the Bible it felfe ; for that oftimes
relates blafphemy not nicely, it defcribes the carnall
fenfe of wicked men not unelegantly, it brings in
holieft men paffionately murmuring againft providence
through all the arguments of *Epicurus:* in other great
difputes it anfwers dubioufly and darkly to the common reader: And afk a Talmudeft what ails the
modefty of his marginall Keri, that *Mofes* and all the
Prophets cannot perfwade him to pronounce the tex-
tuall Chetiv. For thefe caufes we all know the Bible
it felfe put by the Papift into the firft rank of prohibited books. The ancienteft Fathers muft be next
remov'd, as *Clement* of *Alexandria,* and that *Eufebian*
book of Evangelick preparation, tranfmitting our ears
through a hoard of heathenifh obfcenities to receive
the Gofpel. Who finds not that *Irenæus, Epiphanius,
Jerom,* and others difcover more herefies then they
well confute, and that oft for herefie which is the truer
opinion. Nor boots it to fay for thefe, and all the
heathen Writers of greateft infection, if it muft be
thought fo, with whom is bound up the life of human
learning, that they writ in an unknown tongue, fo long

as we are fure thofe languages are known as well
to the worft of men, who are both moft able,
and moft diligent to inftill the poifon they fuck,
firft into the Courts of Princes, acquainting them with
the choiceft delights, and criticifms of fin. As perhaps
did that *Petronius* whom *Nero* call'd his *Arbiter,* the
Mafter of his revels; and that notorious ribald of
Arezzo, dreaded, and yet dear to the Italian Courtiers.
I name not him for pofterities fake, whom *Harry* the
8. nam'd in merriment his Vicar of hell. By which
compendious way all the contagion that foreine books
can infufe, will finde a paffage to the people farre
eafier and fhorter then an Indian voyage, though it
could be fail'd either by the North of *Cataio* Eaftward,
or of *Canada* Weftward, while our Spanifh licencing
gags the Englifh preffe never fo feverely. But on the
other fide that infection which is from books of controverfie in Religion, is more doubtfull and dangerous
to the learned, then to the ignorant; and yet thofe
books muft be permitted untoucht by the licencer. It
will be hard to inftance where any ignorant man hath
bin ever feduc't by Papifticall book in Englifh, unleffe
it were commended and expounded to him by fome of
that Clergy: and indeed all fuch tractats whether
falfe or true are as the Prophefie of *Ifaiah* was to the
Eunuch, not to be *underftood without a guide.* But of
our Priefts and Doctors how many have bin corrupted
by ftudying the comments of Jefuits and *Sorbonifts,*
and how faft they could transfufe that corruption into
the people, our experience is both late and fad. It is
not forgot, fince the acute and .diftinct *Arminius* was
perverted meerly by the perufing of a nameleffe difcours writt'n at *Delf,* which at firft he took in hand to
confute. Seeing therefore that thofe bcoks, and thofe
in great abundance which are likelieft to taint both
life and doctrine, cannot be suppreft without the fall
of learning, and of all ability in difputation, and that
thefe books of either fort are moft and fooneft catch-
ing to the learned, from whom to the common people

what ever is hereticall or diffolute may quickly be con-
vey'd, and that evill manners ε ε as perfectly learnt
without books a thoufand other ways which cannot be
ftopt, and evill doctrine not with books can propagate,
except a teacher guide, which he might alfo doe without writing, and fo beyond prohibiting, I am not able
to unfold, how this cautelous enterprife of licencing
can be exempted from the number of vain and impos-
fible attempts. And he who were pleafantly difpos'd,
could not well avoid to lik'n it to the exploit of that
gallant man who thought to pound up the crows by
fhutting his Parkgate. Befides another inconvenience,
if learned men be the firft receivers out of books and
difpredders both of vice and error, how fhall the
licencers themfelves be confided in, unleffe we can
conferr upon them, or they affume to themfelves above
all others in the Land, the grace of infallibility, and un-
corruptedneffe ? And again if it be true, that a wife man
like a good refiner can gather gold out of the droffieft volume, and that a fool will be a fool with the beft book,
yea or without book, there is no reafon that we fhould
deprive a wife man of any advantage to his wifdome,
while we feek to reftrain from a fool, that which being
reftrain'd will be no hindrance to his folly. For if
there fhould be fo much exactneffe always us'd to
keep that from him which is unfit for his reading, we
fhould in the judgement of *Aristotle* not only, but of
Salomon, and of our Saviour, not voutfafe him good
precepts, and by confequence not willingly admit him
to good books, as being certain that a wife man will
make better ufe of an idle pamphlet, then a fool will
do of facred Scripture. 'Tis next alleg'd we muft not
expofe our felves to temptations without neceffity, and
next to that, not imploy our time in vain things.
To both thefe objections one anfwer will ferve, out
of the grounds already laid, that to all men fuch books
are not temptations, nor vanities ; but ufefull drugs and
materialls wherewith to temper and compofe effective
and ftrong med'cins, which mans life cannot want. The

reſt, as children and childiſh men, who have not the art
to qualifie and prepare theſe working mineralls, well
may be exhorted to forbear, but hinder'd forcibly they
cannot be by all the licencing that Sainted Inquiſition
could ever yet contrive; which is what I promis'd to
deliver next, That this order of licencing conduces
nothing to the end for which it was fram'd; and hath
almoſt prevented me by being clear already while thus
much hath bin explaining. See the ingenuity of Truth,
who when ſhe gets a free and willing hand, opens her
ſelf faſter, then the pace of method and diſcours can
overtake her. It was the taſk which I began with, To
ſhew that no Nation, or well inſtituted State, if they
valu'd books at all, did ever uſe this way of licencing;
and it might be anſwer'd, that this is a piece of prudence lately diſcover'd, To which I return, that as it was
a thing ſlight and obvious to think on, for if it had bin
difficult to finde out, there wanted not among them long
ſince, who ſuggeſted ſuch a cours; which they not following, leave us a pattern of their judgement, that it
was not the not knowing, but the not approving, which
was the cauſe of their not uſing it. *Plato,* a man of
high autority indeed, but leaſt of all for his Commonwealth, in the book of his laws, which no City ever yet
receiv'd, fed his fancie with making many ediĉts to his
ayrie Burgomaſters, which they who otherwiſe admire
him, wiſh had bin rather buried and excus'd in the
genial cups of an *Academick* night-ſitting. By which
laws he ſeems to tolerat no kind of learning, but by
unalterable decree, confiſting moſt of practicall traditions, to the attainment whereof a Library of ſmaller
bulk then his own dialogues would be abundant. And
there alſo enaĉts that no Poet ſhould ſo much as read
to any privat man, what he had writt'n, untill the Judges
and Law-keepers had ſeen it, and allow'd it : But that
Plato meant this Law peculiarly to that Commonwealth
which he had imagin'd, and to no other, is evident.
Why was he not elſe a Law-giver to himſelf, but a
tranſgreſſor, and to be expell'd by his own Magiſtrats;

D

both for the wanton epigrams and dialogues which he
made, and his perpetuall reading of *Sophron Mimus,*
and *Ariſtophanes,* books of groſſeſt infamy, and alſo
for commending ʒhe latter of them though he were
the malicious libeller of his chief friends, to be read
by the Tyrant *Dionyſius,* who had little need of ſuch
traſh to ſpend his time on ? But that he knew this
licencing of Poems had reference and dependence to
many other proviſo's there ſet down in his fancied
republic, which in this world could have no place : and
ſo neither he himſelf, nor any Magiſtrat, or City ever
imitated that cours, which tak'n apart from thoſe
other collaterall injunctions muſt needs be vain and
fruitleſſe. For if they fell upon one kind of ſtrictneſſe,
unleſſe their care were equall to regulat all other things
of like aptnes to corrupt the mind, that ſingle endeavour they knew would be but a fond labour ; to ſhut
and fortifie one gate againſt corruption, and be neceſ-
ſitated to leave others round about wide open. If we
think to regulat Printing, thereby to rectifie manners,
we muſt regulat all recreations and paſtimes, all that is
delightfull to man. No muſick muſt be heard, no ſong
be ſet or ſung, but what is grave and *Dorick.* There
muſt be licencing dancers, that no geſture, motion, or
deportment be taught our youth but what by their allowance ſhall be thought honeſt ; for ſuch *Plato* was
provided of ; It will aſk more then the work of twenty
licencers to examin all the lutes, the violins, and the
ghittarrs in every houſe ; they muſt not be ſuffer'd to
prattle as they doe, but muſt be licenc'd what they may
ſay. And who ſhall ſilence all the airs and madrigalls,
that whiſper ſoftnes in chambers ? The Windows alſo,
and the *Balcone's* muſt be thought on, there are ſhrewd
books, with dangerous Frontiſpices ſet to ſale ; who
ſhall prohibit them, ſhall twenty licencers ? The vil-
lages alſo muſt have their viſitors to enquire what lectures the bagpipe and the rebbeck reads ev'n to the
ballatry, and the gammuth of every *municipal* fidler,
for theſe are the Countrymans *Arcadia's* and his *Monte*

Mayors. Next, what more Nationall corruption, for which England hears ill abroad, then houſhold gluttony; who ſhall be the rectors of our daily rioting? and what ſhall be done to inhibit the multitudes that frequent thoſe houſes where drunk'nes is ſold and harbour'd? Our garments alſo ſhould be referr'd to the licencing of ſome more ſober work-maſters to ſee them cut into a leſſe wanton garb. Who ſhall regulat all the mixt converſation of our youth, male and female together, as is the faſhion of this Country, who ſhall ſtill appoint what ſhall be diſcours'd, what preſum'd, and no furder? Laſtly, who ſhall forbid and ſeparat all idle reſort, all evill company? Theſe things will be, and muſt be; but how they ſhall be left hurtfull, how left enticing, herein conſiſts the grave and governing wiſdom of a State. To ſequeſter out of the world into *Atlantick* and *Eutopian* polities, which never can be drawn into uſe, will not mend our condition; but to ordain wiſely as in this world of evill, in the midd'ſt whereof God hath plac't us unavoidably. Nor is it *Plato's* licencing of books will doe this, which neceſſarily pulls along with it ſo many other kinds of licencing, as will make us all both ridiculous and weary, and yet fuſtrat; but thoſe unwritt'n, or at leaſt unconſtraining laws of vertuous education, religious and civill nurture, which *Plato* there mentions, as the bonds and ligaments of the Commonwealth, the pillars and the ſuſtainers of every writt'n Statute; theſe they be which will bear chief ſway in ſuch matters as theſe, when all licencing will be eaſily eluded. Impunity and remiſſenes, for certain are the bane of a Commonwealth, but here the great art lyes to diſcern in what the law is to bid reſtraint and puniſhment, and in what things perſwaſion only is to work. If every action which is good, or evill in man at ripe years, were to be under pittance, and preſcription, and compulſion, what were vertue but a name, what praiſe could be then due to well-doing, what grammercy to be ſober, juſt, or continent? many there be that complain of divin Providence for ſuffering *Adam* to tranſgreſſe, fooliſh

tongues! when God gave him reafon, he gave him freedom to choofe, for reafon is but choofing; he had bin
elfe a meer artificiall *Adam*, fuch an *Adam* as he is in
the motions. We our felves efteem not of that obedience, or love, or gift, which is of force : God therefore
left him free, fet before him a provoking object, ever
almoft in his eyes herein confifted his merit, herein the
right of his reward, the praife of his abftinence. Wherefore did he creat paffions within us, pleafures round
about us, but that thefe rightly temper'd are the very
ingredients of vertu ? They are not fkilfull confiderers
of human things, who imagin to remove fin by removing the matter of fin ; for, befides that it is a huge heap
increafing under the very act of diminifhing though
fome part of it may for a time be withdrawn from fome
perfons, it cannot from all, in fuch a univerfall thing as
books are ; and when this is done, yet the fin remains
entire. Though ye take from a covetous man all his
treafure, he has yet one jewell left, ye cannot bereave
him of his covetoufneffe. Banifh all objects of luft,
fhut up all youth into the fevereft difcipline that can
be exercis'd in any hermitage, ye cannot make them
chafte, that came not thither fo ; fuch great care and
wifdom is requir'd to the right managing of this point.
Suppofe we could expell fin by this means ; look how
much we thus expell of fin, fo much we expell of vertue : for the matter of them both is the fame ; remove
that, and ye remove them both alike. This juftifies
the high providence of God, who though he command
us temperance, juftice, continence, yet powrs out before
us ev'n to a profufenes all defirable things, and gives
us minds that can wander beyond all limit and fatiety.
Why fhould we then affect a rigor contrary to the manner of God and of nature, by abridging or fcanting
thofe means, which books freely permitted are, both
to the triall of vertue, and the exercife of truth. It
would be better done to learn that the law muft needs
be frivolous which goes to reftrain things, uncertainly
and yet equally working to good, and to evill. And

were I the choofer, a dram of well-doing fhould be preferr'd before many times as much the forcible hindrance
of evill-doing. For God fure efteems the growth and
compleating of one vertuous perfon, more then the
reftraint of ten vitious. And albeit what ever thing we
hear or fee, fitting, walking, travelling, or converfing
may be fitly call'd our book, and is of the fame effect
that writings are, yet grant the thing to be prohibited
were only books, it appears that this order hitherto is
far infufficient to the end which it intends. Do we not
fee, not once or oftner, but weekly that continu'd Court-
libell againft the Parlament and City, Printed, as the
wet fheets can witnes, and difpers't among us for all
that licencing can doe? yet this is the prime fervice a
man would think, wherein this order fhould give proof
of it felf. If it were executed, you'l fay. But certain, if
execution be remiffe or blindfold now, and in this particular, what will it be hereafter, and in other books.
If then the order fhall not be vain and fruftrat, behold
a new labour, Lords and Commons, ye muft repeal and
profcribe all fcandalous and unlicenc't books already
printed and divulg'd; after ye have drawn them up into
a lift, that all may know which are condemn'd, and
which not; and ordain that no forrein books be deliver'd out of cuftody, till they have bin read over. This
office will require the whole time of not a few overfeers,
and thofe no vulgar men. There be alfo books which
are partly ufefull and excellent, partly culpable and
pernicious; this work will afk as many more officials
to make expurgations and expunctions, that the Commonwealth of learning be not damnify'd. In fine, when
the multitude of books encreafe upon their hands, ye
muft be fain to catalogue all thofe Printers who are
found frequently offending, and forbidd the importation
of their whole fufpected *typography.* In a word, that
this your order may be exact, and not deficient, ye muft
reform it perfectly according to the model of *Trent* and
Sevil, which I know ye abhorre to doe. Yet though
ye fhould condifcend to this, which God forbid, the

order ftill would be but fruitleffe and defective to that end whereto ye meant it. If to prevent fects and fchifms, who is fo unread or fo uncatechis'd in ftory, that hath not heard of many fects refuling books as a hindrance, and preferving their doctrine unmixt for many ages, only by unwritt'n traditions. The Chriftian faith, for that was once a fchifm, is not unknown to have fpread all over *Afia*, ere any Gofpel or Epiftle was feen in writing. If the amendment of manners be aym'd at, look into Italy and Spain, whether thofe places be one fcruple the better, the honefter, the wifer, the chafter, fince all the inquifitionall rigor that hath bin executed upon books.

Another reafon, whereby to make it plain that this order will miffe the end it feeks, confider by the quality which ought to be in every licencer. It cannot be deny'd but that he who is made judge to fit upon the birth, or death of books whether they may be wafted into this world, or not, had need to be a man above the common meafure, both ftudious, learned, and judicious ; there may be elfe no mean miftakes in the cenfure of what is paffable or not; which is alfo no mean injury. If he be of fuch worth as behoovs him, there cannot be a more tedious and unpleafing journey-work, a greater loffe of time levied upon his head, then to be made the perpetuall reader of unchofen books and pamphlets, oftimes huge volumes. There is no book that is accept-able unleffe at certain feafons ; but to be enjoyn'd the reading of that at all times, and in a hand fcars legible, whereof three pages would not down at any time in the faireft Print, is an impofition which I cannot beleeve how he that values time, and his own ftudies, or is but of a fenfible noftrill fhould be able to endure. In this one thing I crave leave of the prefent licencers to be pardon'd for fo thinking : who doubleffe took this office up, looking on it through their obedience to the Par-lament, whofe command perhaps made all things feem eafie and unlaborious to them ; but that this fhort triall hath wearied them out already, their own expreffions and excufes to them who make fo many journeys to follicit their licence, are teftimony anough. Seeing therefore thofe who now poffeffe the imployment, by all evident figns wifh themfelves well ridd of it, and that no man of worth, none that is not a plain unthrift of his own hours is ever likely to fucceed them, except he mean to put himfelf to the falary of a Preffe-corrector, we may eafily forefee what kind of licencers we are to expect hereafter, either ignorant, imperious, and remiffe, or bafely pecuniary. This is what I had to fhew wherein this order cannot conduce to that end, whereof it bears the intention.

I laftly proceed from the no good it can do, to the manifeft hurt it caufes, in being firft the greateft difcouragement and affront that can be offer'd to learning and to learned men. It was the complaint and lamentation of Prelats, upon every leaft breath of a motion to remove pluralities, and diftribute more equally Church revennu's, that then all learning would be for ever dafht and difcourag'd. But as for that opinion, I never found caufe to think that the tenth part of learning ftood or fell with the Clergy : nor could I ever but hold it for a fordid and unworthy fpeech of any Churchman who had a competency left him. If therefore ye be loath to difhearten utterly and difcontent, not the mercenary crew of falfe pretenders to learning, but the free and ingenuous fort of fuch as evidently were born to ftudy, and love lerning for it felf, not for lucre, or any other end, but the fervice of God and of truth, and perhaps that lafting fame and perpetuity of praife which God and good men have confented fhall be the reward of thofe whofe publifht labours advance the good of mankind, then know, that fo far to diftruft the judgement and the honefty of one who hath but a common repute in learning, and never yet offended, as not to count him fit to print his mind without a tutor and examiner, left he fhould drop a fcifm, or fomething of corruption, is the greateft difpleafure and indignity to a free and knowing fpirit that can be put upon him. What advantage is it to be a man over it is to be a boy at fchool, if we have only fcapt the

ferular, to come under the fefcu of an *Imprimatur*? if
ferious and elaborat writings, as if they were no more
then the theam of a Grammar lad under his Pedagogue
muft not be utter'd without the curfory eyes of a tem-
porizing and extemporizing licencer. He who is not
trufted with his own actions, his drift not being known
to be evill, and ftanding to the hazard of law and penalty,
has no great argument to think himfelf reputed in the
Commonwealth wherein he was born, for other then a
fool or a foreiner. When a man writes to the world,
he fummons up all his reafon and deliberation to affift
him; he fearches, meditats, is induftrious, and likely
confults and conferrs with his judicious friends; after
all which done he takes himfelf to be inform'd in what
he writes, as well as any that writ before him; if in this
the moft confummat act of his fidelity and ripeneffe, no
years, no induftry, no former proof of his abilities can
bring him to that ftate of maturity, as not to be ftill
miftrufted and fufpected, unleffe he carry all his confiderat diligence, all his midnight watchings, and expence
of *Palladian* oyl, to the hafty view of an unleafur'd
licencer, perhaps much his younger, perhaps far his in-
feriour in judgement, perhaps one who never knew the
labour of book-writing, and if he be not repulft, or
flighted, muft appear in Print like a punie with his
guardian, and his cenfors hand on the back of his title
to be his bayl and furety, that he is no idiot, or feducer,
it cannot be but a difhonor and derogation to the author,
to the book, to the priviledge and dignity of Learning.
And what if the author fhall be one fo copious of fancie,
as to have many things well worth the adding, come
into his mind after licencing, while the book is yet under
the Preffe, which not feldom happ'ns to the beft and
diligenteft writers; and that perhaps a dozen times in
one book. The Printer dares not go beyond his licenc't
copy; fo often then muft the author trudge to his leav-
giver, that thofe his new infertions may be viewd; and
many a jaunt will be made, ere that licencer, for it muft
be the fame man, can either be found, or found at leifure;

mean while either the Preſſe muſt ſtand ſtill, which is
no ſmall damage, or the author looſe his accurateſt
thoughts, and ſend the book forth wors then he had
made it, which to a diligent writer is the greateſt melan-
choly and vexation that can befall. And how can a
man teach with autority, which is the life of teaching,
how can he be a Doctor in his book as he ought to be,
or elſe had better be ſilent, whenas all he teaches, all he
delivers, is but under the tuition, under the correction
of his patriarchal licencer to blot or alter what preciſely
accords not with the hidebound humor which he calls
his judgement. When every acute reader upon the firſt
ſight of a pedantick licence, will be ready with theſe like
words to ding the book a coits diſtance from him, I hate
a pupil teacher, I endure not an inſtructer that comes
to me under the wardſhip of an overſeeing fiſt. I know
nothing of the licencer, but that I have his own hand
here for his arrogance ; who ſhall warrant me his judgement? The State Sir, replies the Stationer, but has a
quick return, The State ſhall be my governours, but not
my criticks ; they may be miſtak'n in the choice of a
licencer, as eaſily as this licencer may be miſtak'n in an
author : This is ſome common ſtuffe ; and he might
adde from Sir *Francis Bacon*, That *ſuch authoriz'd books
are but the language of the times.* For though a licencer
ſhould happ'n to be judicious more then ordnary, which
will be a great jeopardy of the next ſucceſſion, yet his
very office, and his commiſſion enjoyns him to let paſſe
nothing but what is vulgarly receiv'd already. Nay, which
is more lamentable, if the work of any deceaſed author,
though never ſo famous in his life time, and even to this
day, come to their hands for licence to be Printed, or
Reprinted, if there be found in his book one ſentence
of a ventrous edge, utter'd in the height of zeal, and who
knows whether it might not be the dictat of a divine
Spirit, yet not ſuiting with every low decrepit humor of
their own, though it were *Knox* himſelf, the Reformer
of a Kingdom that ſpake it, they will not pardon him their
daſh : the ſenſe of that great man ſhall to all poſterity be

loft, for the fearfulneffe, or the prefumptuous rafhneffe
of a perfunctory licencer. And to what an author this
violence hath bin lately done, and in what book of greateft confequence to be faithfully publifht, I could now
inftance, but fhall forbear till a more convenient feafon.
Yet if thefe things be not refented ferioufly and timely
by them who have the remedy in their power, but that
fuch iron moulds as thefe fhall have autority to knaw
out the choifeft periods of exquifiteft books, and to commit fuch a treacherous fraud againft the orphan remain-
ders of worthieft men after death, the more forrow will
belong to that haples race of men, whofe misfortune it
is to have underftanding. Henceforth let no man care
to learn, or care to be more then worldly wife ; for certainly in higher matters to be ignorant and flothfull, to
be a common ftedfaft dunce will be the only pleafant
life, and only in requeft.

And as it is a particular difefteem of every knowing
perfon alive, and moft injurious to the writt'n labours
and monuments of the dead, fo to me it feems an un-
dervaluing and vilifying of the whole Nation. I cannot
fet fo light by all the invention, the art, the wit, the
grave and folid judgement which is in England, as that
it can be comprehended in any twenty capacities how
good foever, much leffe that it fhould not paffe except
their fuperintendence be over it, except it be fifted and
ftrain'd with their ftrainers, that it fhould be uncurrant
without their manuall ftamp. Truth and underftanding
are not fuch wares as to be monopoliz'd and traded in
by tickets and ftatutes, and ftandards. We muft not
think to make a ftaple commodity of all the knowledge
in the Land, to mark and licence it like our broad
cloath, and our wooll packs. What is it but a fervi-
tude like that impos'd by the Philiftims, not to be
allow'd the fharpning of our own axes and coulters,
but we muft repair from all quarters to twenty licencing
forges. Had any one writt'n and divulg'd erroneous
things and fcandalous to honeft life, mifufing and forfeiting the efteem had of his reafon among men, if

after conviction this only cenfure were adjudg'd him, that he fhould never henceforth write, but what were firft examin'd by an appointed officer, whofe hand fhould be annext to paffe his credit for him, that now he might be fafely read, it could not be apprehend leffe then a difgracefull punifhment. Whence to include the whole Nation, and thofe that never yet thus offended, under fuch a diffident and fufpectfull prohibition, may plainly be underftood what a difparagement it is. So much the more, when as dettors and delinquents may walk abroad without a keeper, but unoffenfive books muft not ftirre forth without a vifible jaylor in thir title. Nor is it to the common people leffe then a reproach ; for if we fo jealous over them, as that we dare not truft them with an Englifh pamphlet, what doe we but cen-fure them for a giddy, vitious, and ungrounded people ; in fuch a fick and weak eftate of faith and difcretion, as to be able to take nothing down but through the pipe of a licencer. That this is care or love of them, we cannot pretend, whenas in thofe Popifh places where the Laity are moft hated and defpis'd the fame ftrictnes is us'd over them. Wifdom we cannot call it, becaufe it ftops but one breach of licence, nor that neither ; whenas thofe corruptions which it feeks to prevent, break in fafter at other dores which cannot be fhut.

And in conclufion it reflects to the difrepute of our Minifters alfo, of whofe labours we fhould hope better, and of the proficiencie which thir flock reaps by them, then that after all this light of the Gofpel which is, and is to be, and all this continuall preaching, they fhould be ftill frequented with fuch an unprincipl'd, unedi-fy'd, and laick rabble, as that the whiffe of every new pamphlet fhould ftagger them out of their catechifm, and Chriftian walking. This may have much reafon to difcourage the Minifters when fuch a low conceit is had of all their exhortations, and the benefiting of their hearers, as that they are not thought fit to be turn'd loofe to three fheets of paper without a licencer, that all the Sermons, all the Lectures preacht, printed, vented in fuch numbers, and fuch volumes, as have now wellnigh made all other books unfalable, fhould not be armor anough againft one fingle *enchiridion*, without the caftle of St *Angelo* of an *Imprimatur.*

And left fom fhould perfwade ye, Lords and Commons, that thefe arguments of lerned mens difcouragement at this your order, are meer flourifhes, and not reall, I could recount what I have feen and heard in other Countries, where this kind of inquifition tyrannizes; when I have fat among their lerned men, for. that honor I had, and bin counted happy to be born in fuch a place of *Philofophic* freedom, as they fuppos'd England was, while themfelvs did nothing but bemoan the fervil condition into which lerning amongft them was brought; that this was it which had dampt the glory of Italian wits; that nothing had bin there writt'n now thefe many years but flattery and fuftian. There it was that I found and vifited the famous *Galileo* grown old, a prifner to the Inquifition, for thinking in Aftronomy otherwife then the Francifcan and Dominican licencers thought. And though I knew that England then was groaning loudeft under the Prelaticall yoak, nevertheleffe I tooke it as a pledge of future happines, that other Nations were fo perfwaded of her liberty. Yet was it beyond my hope that thofe Worthies were then breathing in her air, who fhould be her leaders to fuch a deliverance, as fhall never be forgott'n by any revolution of time that this world hath to finifh. When that was once begun, it was as little in my fear, that what words of complaint I heard among lerned men of other parts utter'd againft the Inquifition, the fame I fhould hear by as lerned men at home utterd in time of Parlament againft an order of licencing; and that fo generally, that when I difclos'd my felf a companion of their difcontent, I might fay, if without envy, that he whom an honeft *quæftorfhip* had indear'd to the *Sicilians*, was not more by them importun'd againft *Verres*, then the favourable opinion which I had among many who honour ye, and are known and

respected by ye, loaded me with entreaties and per-
fwafions, that I would not defpair to lay together that
which juft reafon fhould bring into my mind, toward
the removal of an undeferved thraldom upon lerning.
That this is not therefore the disburdning of a particular fancie, but the common grievance of all thofe
who had prepar'd their minds and ftudies above the
vulgar pitch to advance truth in others, and from others
to entertain it, thus much may fatisfie. And in their
name I fhall for neither friend nor foe conceal what
the generall murmur is ; that if it come to inquifitioning
again, and licencing, and that we are fo timorous of
our felvs, and fo fufpicious of all men, as to fear each
book, and the fhaking of every leaf, before we know
what the contents are, if fome who but of late were
little better then filenc't from preaching, fhall come
now to filence us from reading, except what they pleafe,
it cannot be gueft what is intended by fom but a fecond
tyranny over learning : and will foon put it out of controverfie that Bifhops and Prefbyters are the fame to
us both name and thing. That thofe evills of Prelaty
which before from five or fix and twenty Sees were dif-
tributivly charg'd upon the whole people, will now light
wholly upon learning, is not obfcure to us : whenas
now the Paftor of a fmall unlearned Parifh, on the fudden fhall be exalted Archbifhop over a large dioces of
books, and yet not remove, but keep his other cure
too, a myfticall pluralift. He who but of late cry'd
down the fole ordination of every novice Batchelor of
Art, and deny'd fole jurifdiction over the fimpleft Pa-
rifhioner, fhall now at home in his privat chair affume
both thefe over worthieft and excellenteft books and
ableft authors that write them. This is not, Yee
Covenants and Proteftations that we have made, this
is not to put down Prelaty, this is but to chop an
Epifcopacy, this is but to tranflate the Palace *Metro-*
politan from one kind of dominion into another, this
is but an old cannonicall flight of *commuting* our
penance. To ftartle thus betimes at a meer unlicenc't

pamphlet will after a while be afraid of every conventicle, and a while after will make a conventicle of every Chriftian meeting. But I am certain that a State govern'd by the rules of juftice and fortitude, or a Church built and founded upon the rock of faith and true knowledge, cannot be fo pufillanimous. While things are yet not conftituted in Religion, that freedom of writing fhould be reftrain'd by a difcipline imitated from the Prelats, and learnt by them from the Inquifition to fhut us up all again into the breft of a licencer, muft needs give caufe of doubt and difcouragement to all learned and religious men. Who cannot but difcern the finenes of this politic drift, and who are the contrivers; that while Bifhops were to be baited down, then all Preffes might be open; it was the people's birthright and priviledge in time of Parlament, it was the breaking forth of light. But now the Bifhops abrogated and voided out of the Church, as if our Reformation fought no more, but to make room for others into their feats under another name, the Epifcopall arts begin to bud again, the crufe of truth muft run no more oyle, liberty of Printing muft be enthrall'd again under a Prelaticall commiffion of twenty, the privilege of the people nullify'd, and which is wors, the freedom of learning muft groan again, and to her old fetters; all this the Parlament yet fitting. Although their own late arguments and defences againft the Prelats might remember them that this obftructing violence meets for the moft part with an event utterly oppofite to the end which it drives at : inftead of fuppreffing fects and fchifms, it raifes them and invefts them with a reputation : *The punifhing of wits enhaunces their autority*, faith the Vicount St. *Albans, and a forbidd'n writing is thought to be a certain fpark of truth that flies up in the faces of them who feeke to tread it out.* This order therefore may prove a nurfing mother to fects, but I fhall eafily fhew how it will be a ftep-dame to Truth : and firft by difinabling us to the maintenance of what is known already.

    Well knows he who ufes to confider, that our faith

and knowledge thrives by exercife, as well as our limbs and complexion. Truth is compar'd in Scripture to a ftreaming fountain ; if her waters flow not in a perpetuall progreffion, they fick'n into a muddy pool of conformity and tradition. A man may be a heretick in the truth ; and if he beleeve things only becaufe his Paftor fayes fo, or the Affembly fo determins, without knowing other reafon, though his belief be true, yet the very truth he holds, becomes his herefie. There is not any burden that fom would gladier poft off to another, then the charge and care of their Religion. There be, who knows not that there be of Proteftants and profeffors who live and dye in as arrant an implicit faith, as any lay Papift of Loretto. A wealthy man addicted to his pleafure and to his profits, finds Religion to be a traffick fo entangl'd, and of fo many piddling accounts, that of all myfteries he cannot fkill to keep a ftock going upon that trade. What fhoulde he doe ? fain he would have the name to be religous, fain he would bear up with his neighbours in that. What does he therefore, but refolvs to give over toyling, and to find himfelf out fom factor, to whofe care and credit he may commit the whole managing of his religous affairs ; fom Divine of note and eftimation that muft be. To him he adheres, refigns the whole ware-houfe of his religion, with all the locks and keyes into his cuftody ; and indeed makes the very perfon of that man his religion ; efteems his affociating with him a fufficient evidence and commendatory of his own piety. So that a man may fay his religion is now no more within himfelf, but is becom a dividuall movable, and goes and comes neer him, according as that good man frequents the houfe. He entertains him, gives him gifts, feafts him, lodges him ; his religion comes home at night, praies, is liberally fupt, and fumptuoufly laid to fleep, rifes, is faluted, and after the malmfey, or fome well fpic't bruage, and better breakfafted then he whofe morning appetite would have gladly fed on green figs between *Bethany* and *Ierufalem*, his Religion walks abroad at eight. and

leavs his kind entertainer in the fhop trading all day
without his religion.

Another fort there be who when they hear that all
things fhall be order'd, all things regulated and fetl'd;
nothing writt'n but what paffes through the cuftom-
houfe of certain Publicans that have the tunaging and
the poundaging of all free fpok'n truth, will ftrait give
themfelvs up into your hands, mak'em and cut'em out
what religion ye pleafe; there be delights, there be
recreations and jolly paftimes that will fetch the day
about from fun to fun, and rock the tedious year as
in a delightfull dream. What need they torture their
heads with that which others have tak'n fo ftrictly, and
fo unalterably into their own pourveying. Thefe are
the fruits which a dull eafe and ceffation of our knowledge will bring forth among the people. How goodly,
and how to be wifht were fuch an obedient unanimity
as this, what a fine conformity would it ftarch us all
into? doubtles a ftanch and folid peece of framework, as any January could freeze together.

Nor much better will be the confequence ev'n among
the Clergy themfelvs; it is no new thing never heard
of before, for a *parochiall* Minifter, who has his reward,
and is at his *Hercules* pillars in a warm benefice, to be
eafily inclinable, if he have nothing elfe that may roufe
up his ftudies, to finifh his circuit in an Englifh con-
cordance and a *topic folio*, the gatherings and favings
of a fober graduatfhip, a *Harmony* and a *Catena*,
treading the conftant round of certain common doc-
trinall heads, attended with their ufes, motives, marks
and means, out of which as out of an alphabet or fol
fa by forming and transforming, joyning and dif-
joyning varioufly a little book-craft, and two hours
meditation might furnifh him unspeakably to the per-
formance of more then a weekly charge of fermoning :
not to reck'n up the infinit helps of interlinearies,
breviaries, *fynopfes*, and other loitering gear. But as
for the multitude of Sermons ready printed and pil'd
up, on every text that is not difficult, our London

trading St *Thomas* in his veftry, and adde to boot St. *Martin*, and St *Hugh*, have not within their hallow'd limits more vendible ware of all forts ready made : fo that penury he never need fear of Pulpit provifion, having where fo plenteoufly to refrefh his magazin. But if his rear and flanks be not impal'd, if his back dore be not fecur'd by the rigid licencer, but that a bold book may now and then iffue forth, and give the affault to fome of his old collections in their trenches, it will concern him then to keep waking, to ftand in watch, to fet good guards and fentinells about his receiv'd opinions, to walk the round and counter-round with his fellow infpectors, fearing leaft any of his flock be feduc't, who alfo then would be better inftructed, better exercis'd and difciplin'd. And God fend that the fear of this diligence which muft then be us'd, doe not make us affect the lazines of a licencing Church.

For if we be fure we are in the right, and doe not hold the truth guiltily, which becomes not, if we ourfelves condemn not our own weak and frivolous teaching, and the people for an untaught and irreligious gadding rout, what can be more fair, then when a man judicious, learned, and of a confcience, for ought we know, as good as theirs that taught us what we know, fhall not privily from houfe to houfe, which is more dangerous, but openly by writing publifh to the world what his opinion is, what his reafons, and wherefore that which is now thought cannot be found. Chrift urg'd it as wherewith to juftifie himfelf, that he preacht in publick; yet writing is more publick then preaching; and more eafie to refutation, if need be, there being fo many whofe bufineffe and profeffion meerly it is, to be the champions of Truth ; which if they neglect, what can be imputed but their floth, or inabilty ?

Thus much we are hinder'd and dif-inur'd by this cours of licencing towards the true knowledge of what we feem to know. For how much it hurts and hinders the licencers themfelves in the calling of their Miniftery, more then any fecular employment, if they will difcharge that office as they ought, fo that of neceffity they muft neglect either the one duty or the other, I infift not, becaufe it is a particular, but leave it to their own confcience, how they will decide it there.

There is yet behind of what I purpos'd to lay open, the incredible loffe, and detriment that this plot of licencing puts us to, more then if fom enemy at fea fhould ftop up all our hav'ns and ports, and creeks, it hinders and retards the importation of our richeft Marchandize, Truth ; nay it was firft eftablifht and put in practice by Antichriftian malice and myftery on fet purpofe to extinguifh, if it were poffible, the light of Reformation, and to fettle falfhood ; little differing from that policie wherewith the Turk upholds his *Alcoran*, by the prohibition of Printing. 'Tis not deny'd, but gladly confeft, we are to fend our thanks and vows to heav'n, louder then moft of Nations, for that great mea-fure of truth which we enjoy, efpecially in thofe main points between us and the Pope, with his appertinences the Prelats : but he who thinks we are to pitch our tent here, and have attain'd the utmoft prospect of reforma-tion, that the mortalle glaffe wherein we contemplate, can fhew us, till we come to *beatific* vifion, that man by this very opinion declares, that he is yet farre fhort of Truth.

Truth indeed came once into the world with her divine Mafter, and was a perfect fhape moft glorious to look on : but when he afcended, and his Apoftles after him were laid afleep, then ftrait arofe a wicked race of deceivers, who as that ftory goes of the *Ægyptian Typhon* with his confpirators, how they dealt with the good *Ofiris*, took the virgin Truth, hewd her lovely form into a thoufand peeces, and fcatter'd them to the four winds. From that time ever fince, the fad friends of Truth, fuch as durft appear, imitating the carefull fearch that *Ifis* made for the mangl'd body of *Ofiris*, went up and down gathering up limb by limb ftill as they could find them. We have not yet found them all, Lords and Commons, nor ever fhall doe, till her Mafters fecond comming; he fhall bring together every joynt and member, and fhall mould them into an immortall feature of lovelinefs and perfection. Suffer not thefe licencing prohibitions to ftand at every place of opportunity forbidding and difturbing them that continue feeking, that continue to do our obfequies to the torn body of our martyr'd Saint. We boaft our light; but if we look not wifely on the Sun it felf, it fmites us into darknes. Who can difcern thofe planets that are oft *Combuft*, and thofe ftars of brighteft magnitude that rife and fet with the Sun, untill the oppofite motion of their orbs bring them to fuch a place in the firmament, where they may be feen evning or morning. The light which we have gain'd, was giv'n us, not to be ever ftaring on, but by it to difcover onward things more remote from our knowledge. It is not the unfrocking of a Prieft, the unmitring of a Bifhop, and the removing him from off the *Prefbyterian* fhoulders that will make us a happy Nation, no, if other things as great in the Church, and in the rule of life both economicall and politicall be not lookt into and reform'd, we have lookt fo long upon the blaze that *Zuinglius* and *Calvin* hath beacon'd up to us, that we are ftark blind. There be who perpetually complain of fchifms and fects, and make it fuch a calamity that any man diffents from their maxims. 'Tis their own pride and ignorance which caufes the difturbing, who neither will hear with meeknes, nor can convince, yet all muft be fuppreft which is not found in their *Syntagma*. They are the troublers, they are the dividers of unity, who neglect and permit not others to unite thofe diffever'd peeces which are yet wanting to the body of Truth. To be ftill fearching what we know not, by what we know, ftill clofing up truth to truth as we find it (for all her body is *homogeneal*, and proportionall) this is the golden rule in *Theology* as well as in Arithmetick, and makes up the beft harmony in a Church; not the forc't and outward union of cold, and neutrall, and inwardly divided minds.

Lords and Commons of England, confider what Nation it is wherof ye are, and wherof ye are the governours : a Nation not flow and dull, but of a quick, ingenious, and piercing fpirit, acute to invent, futtle and finewy to difcours, not beneath the reach of any point the higheſt that human capacity can foar to. Therefore the ſtudies of learning in her deepeſt Sciences have bin fo ⸳ncient, and fo eminent among us, that Writers of good antiquity, and ableſt judgement have bin perfwaded that ev'n the fchool of *Pythagoras*, and the *Perſian* wifdom took beginning from the old Philofophy of this Iland.　And that wife and civill Roman, *Julius Agricola*, who govern'd once here for *Cæſar*, preferr'd the naturall wits of Britain, before the labour'd ſtudies of the French.　Nor is it for nothing that the grave and frugal *Tranſilvanian* fends out yearly from as farre as the mountanous borders of *Ruſſia*, and beyond the *Hercynian* wildernes, not their youth, but their ſtay'd men, to learn our language, and our *theologic* arts.　Yet that which is above all this, the favour and the love of heav'n we have great argument to think in a peculiar manner propitious and propending towards us.　Why elfe was this Nation chos'n before any other, that out of her as out of *Sion* fhould be proclam'd and founded forth the firſt tidings and trumpet of Reformation to all *Europ.*　And had it not bin the obſtinat perverfnes of our Prelats againſt the divine and admirable fpirit of *Wicklef*, to fuppreffe him as a fchifmatic and *innovator*, perhaps neither the *Bohemian Huſſe* and *Jerom*, no nor the name of *Luther*, or of *Calvin* had bin ever known : the glory of reforming all our neighbours had bin compleatly ours.　But now, as our obdurat Clergy have with violence demean'd the matter, we are become hitherto the lateſt and the backwardeſt Schollers, of whom God offer'd to have made us the teachers.　Now once again by all concurrence of figns, and by the generall inſtinct of holy and devout men, as they daily and folemnly expreffe their thoughts, God is decreeing to begin fome new and great period in his Church, ev'n to the reform-

ing of Reformation it felf: what does he then but
reveal Himfelf to his fervants, and as his manner is,
firft to his Englifh-men ; I fay as his manner is, firft
to us, though we mark not the method of his counfels,
and are unworthy. Behold now this vaft City ; a City
of refuge, the manfion houfe of liberty, encompaft and
furrounded with his protection ; the fhop of warre hath
not there more anvils and hammers waking, to fafhion
out the plates and inftruments of armed Juftice in
defence of beleaguer'd Truth, then there be pens and
heads there, fitting by their ftudious lamps, mufing,
fearching, revolving new notions and idea's wherewith
to prefent, as with their homage and their fealty the
approaching Reformation : others as faft reading, trying
all things, affenting to the force of reafon and convincement. What could a man require more from a Nation
fo pliant and fo prone to feek after knowledge. What
wants there to fuch a towardly and pregnant foile, but
wife and faithfull labourers, to make a knowing people,
a Nation of Prophets, of Sages, and of Worthies. We
reck'n more then five months yet to harveft ; there need
not be five weeks, had we but eyes to lift up, the fields
are white already. Where there is much defire to learn,
there of neceffity will be much arguing, much writing,
many opinions ; for opinion in good men is but knowledge in the making. Under thefe fantaftic terrors of
sect and fchifm, we wrong the earneft and zealous thirft
after knowledge and underftanding which God hath
ftirr'd up in this City. What fome lament of, we rather
fhould rejoyce at, fhould rather praife this pious forwardnes among men, to reaffume the ill deputed care
of their Religion into their own hands again. A little
generous prudence, a little forbearance of one another,
and fom grain of charity might win all thefe diligences
to joyn, and unite in one generall and brotherly fearch
after Truth ; could we but forgoe this Prelaticall tradition of crowding free confciences and Chriftian liberties
into canons and precepts of men. I doubt not, if fome
great and worthy ftranger fhould come among us, wife

to difcern the mould and temper of a people, and how to govern it, obferving the high ʼropes and aims, the diligent alacrity of our extended thoughts and reafonings in the purfuance of truth and freedom, but that he would cry out as *Pirrhus* did, admiring the Roman docility and courage, if fuch were my *Epirots*, I would not defpair the greateft defign that could be attempted to make a Church or Kingdom happy.　Yet thefe are the men cry'd out againft for fchifmaticks and fectaries; as if, while the Temple of the Lord was building, fome cutting, fome fquaring the marble, others hewing the cedars, there fhould be a fort of irrationall men who could not confider there muft be many fchifms and many diffections made in the quarry and in the timber, ere the houfe of God can be built.　And when every ftone is laid artfully together, it cannot be united into a continuity, it can but be contiguous in this world; neither can every peece of the building be of one form ; nay rather the perfection confifts in this, that out of many moderat varieties and brotherly diffimilitudes that are not vaftly difproportionall arifes the goodly and the gracefull fymmetry that commends the whole pile and ftructure.　Let us therefore be more confiderat builders, more wife in fpirituall architecture, when great reformation is expected.　For now the time feems come, wherein *Mofes* the great Prophet may fit in heav'n rejoycing to fee that memorable and glorious wifh of his fulfill'd, when not only our fev'nty Elders, but all the Lords people are become Prophets.　No marvell then though fome men, and fome good men too perhaps, but young in goodneffe, as *Jofhua* then was, envy them. They fret, and out of their own weaknes are in agony, left thofe divifions and fubdivifions will undoe us.　The adverfarie again applauds, and waits the hour, when they have brancht themfelves out, faith he, fmall anough into parties and partitions, then will be our time.　Fool! he fees not the firm root, out of which we all grow, though into branches : nor will beware untill hee fee our fmall divided maniples cutting through at every angle

of his ill united and unweildy brigade. And that we
are to hope better of all thefe fuppofed fects and fchifms,
and that we fhall not need that folicitude honeft perhaps
though over timorous of them that vex in his behalf,
but fhall laugh in the end, at thofe malicious applauders
of our differences, I have thefe reafons to perfwade me.

Firft, when a City fhall be as it were befieg'd and
blockt about; her navigable river infefted, inrodes and
incurfions round, defiance and battell oft rumor'd to
be marching up ev'n to her walls, and fuburb trenches,
that then the people, or the greater part, more then
at other times, wholly tak'n up with the ftudy of
higheft and moft important matters to be reform'd,
fhould be difputing, reafoning, reading, inventing, dif-
courfing, ev'n to a rarity, and admiration, things not
before difcourft or writt'n of, argues firft a fingular
good will, contentedneffe and confidence in your prudent forefight, and fafe government, Lords and Commons ; and from thence derives it felf to a gallant
bravery and well grounded contempt of their enemies,
as if there were no fmall number of as great fpirits
among us, as his was, who when Rome was nigh befieg'd by *Hanibal*, being in the City, bought that peece
of ground at no cheap rate, whereon *Hanibal* himfelf
encampt his own regiment. Next it is a lively and
cherfull prefage of our happy fucceffe and victory.
For as in a body, when the blood is frefh, the fpirits
pure and vigorous, not only to vital, but to rationall
faculties, and thofe in the acuteft, and the perteft
operations of wit and futtlety, it argues in what good
plight and conftitution the body is, fo when the cheer-
fulneffe of the people is fo fprightly up, as that it has,
not only wherewith to guard well its own freedom and
fafety, but to fpare, and to beftow upon the folideft
and fublimeft points of controverfie, and new invention, it betok'n us not degenerated, nor drooping to a
fatall decay, but cafting off the old and wrincl'd fkin
of corruption to outlive thefe pangs and wax young
again, entring the glorious waies of Truth and profpe-

rous vertue deſtin'd to become great and honourable in theſe latter ages. Methinks I ſee in my mind a noble and puiſſant Nation rouſing herſelf like a ſtrong man after ſleep, and ſhaking her invincible locks : Methinks I ſee her as an Eagle muing her mighty youth, and kindling her undazl'd eyes at the full mid-day beam ;. purging and unſcaling her long abuſed ſight at the fountain it ſelf of heav'nly radiance, while the whole noiſe of timorous and flocking birds, with thoſe alſo that love the twilight, flutter about, amaz'd at what ſhe means, and in their envious gabble would prognoſticat a year of ſects and ſchiſms.

What ſhould ye doe then, ſhould ye ſuppreſſe all this flowry crop of knowledge and new light ſprung up and yet ſpringing daily in this City, ſhould ye ſet an *Oligarchy* of twenty ingroſſers over it, to bring a famin upon our minds again, when we ſhall know nothing but what is meaſur'd to us by their buſhel ? Beleeve it, Lords and Commons, they who counſell ye to ſuch a ſuppreſſing, doe as good as bid ye ſuppreſſe your-ſelves ; and I will ſoon ſhew how. If it be deſir'd to know the immediat cauſe of all this free writing and free ſpeaking, there cannot be aſſign'd a truer then your own mild, and free, and human government ; it is the liberty, Lords and Commons, which your own valorous and happy counſels have purchaſt us, liberty which is the nurſe of all great wits ; this is that which hath rarify'd and enlightn'd our ſpirits like the influence of heav'n ; this is that which hath enfranchis'd, enlarg'd and lifted up our apprehenſions degrees above them-ſelves. Ye cannot make us now leſſe capable, leſſe knowing, leſſe eagarly purſuing of the truth, unleſſe ye firſt make your ſelves, that made us ſo, leſſe the lovers, leſſe the founders of our true liberty. We can grow ignorant again, brutiſh, formall, and ſlaviſh, as ye found us ; but you then muſt firſt become that which ye cannot be, oppreſſive, arbitrary, and tyrannous, as they were from whom ye have free'd us. That our hearts are now more capacious, our thoughts more erected to the fearch and expectation of greateſt and exacteſt things, is the iſſue of your owne vertu propagated in us ; ye cannot fuppreſſe that unleſſe ye reinforce an abrogated and mercileſſe law, that fathers may diſpatch at will their own children. And who ſhall then ſticke cloſeſt to ye, and excite others ? not he who takes up armes for cote and conduct, and his four nobles of Danegelt. Although I diſpraiſe not the defence of juſt immunities, yet love my peace better, if that were all. Give me the liberty to know, to utter, and to argue freely according to confcience, above all liberties.

What would be best advis'd then, if it be found ſo hurtfull and ſo unequall to fuppreſſe opinions for the newnes, or the unfutablenes to a cuſtomary acceptance, will not be my taſk to ſay ; I only ſhall repeat what I have learnt from one of your own honourable number, a right noble and pious lord, who had he not facrific'd his life and fortunes to the Church and Commonwealth, we had not now miſt and bewayl'd a worthy and undoubted patron of this argument. Ye know him I am fure ; yet I for honours fake, and may it be eternall to him, ſhall name him, the Lord *Brook.*[5] He writing of Epiſcopacy, and by the way treating of ſects and ſchiſms, left Ye his vote, or rather now the laſt words of his dying charge, which I know will ever be of dear and honour'd regard with Ye, ſo full of meeknes and breathing charity, that next to his laſt teſtament, who bequeath'd love and peace to his Diſciples, I cannot call to mind where I have read or heard words more mild and peacefull. He there exhorts us to hear with patience and humility thoſe, however they be miſcall'd, that deſire to live purely, in ſuch a uſe of Gods Ordinances, as the beſt guidance of their confcience gives them, and to tolerat them, though in ſome diſconformity to our ſelves. The book it ſelf will tell us more at large being publiſht to the world, and dedicated to the Parlament by him who both for his life and for his death deſerves, that what advice he left be not laid by without peruſall.

And now the time in fpeciall is, by priviledge to wrtie and fpeak what may help to the furder difcuffing of matters in agitation. The Temple of *Janus* with his two *controverfal* faces might now not unfignificantly be fet open. And though all the windes of doctrin were let loofe to play upon the earth, fo Truth be in the field, we do injurioufly by licencing and prohibiting to mifdoubt her ftrength. Let her and Falfhood grapple ; who ever knew Truth put to the wors, in a free and open encounter. Her confuting is the beft and fureft fuppreffing. He who hears what praying there is for light and clearer knowledge to be fent down among us, would think of other matters to be conftituted beyond the difcipline of *Geneva*, fram'd and fabric't already to our hands. Yet when the new light which we beg for fhines in upon us, there be who envy, and oppofe, if it come not firft in at their cafements. What a collufion is this, whenas we are exhorted by the wife man to ufe diligence, *to feek for wifdom as for hidd'n treafures* early and late, that another order fhall enjoyn us to know nothing but by ftatute. When a man hath bin labouring the hardeft labour in the deep mines of knowledge, hath furnifht out his findings in all their equipage, drawn forth his reafons as it were a battell raung'd, fcatter'd and defeated all objections in his way, calls out his adverfary into the plain, offers him the advantage of wind and fun, if he pleafe ; only that he may try the matter by dint of argument, for his opponents then to fculk, to lay ambufhments, to keep a narrow bridge of licencing where the challenger fhould paffe, though it be valour anough in fhouldierfhip, is but weaknes and cowardife in the wars of Truth. For who knows not that Truth is ftrong next to the Almighty ; fhe needs no policies, no ftrategems, no licencings to make her victorious, thofe are the fhifts and the defences that error ufes againft her power : give her but room, and do not bind her when fhe fleeps, for then fhe fpeaks not true, as the old *Proteus* did, who fpake oracles

only when he was caught and bound, but then rather
fhe turns herfelf into all fhapes, except her own, and
perhaps tunes her voice according to the time, as
Micaiah did before Ahab, untill fhe be adjur'd into
her own likenes. Yet is it not impoffible that fhe may
have more fhapes then one. What elfe is all that rank
of things indifferent, wherein Truth may be on this fide,
or on the other, without being unlike her felf. What
but a vain fhadow elfe is the abolition of *thofe ordinances, that hand writing nayl'd to the croffe,* what
great purchafe is this Chriftian liberty which *Paul* fo
often boafts of. His doctrine is, that he who eats or
eats not, regards a day, or regards it not, may doe
either to the Lord. How many other things might be
tolerated in peace, and left to confcience, had we but
charity, and were it not the chiefftrong hold of our
hypocrifie to be ever judging one another. I fear yet
this iron yoke of outward conformity hath left a flavifh
print upon our necks ; the ghoft of a linnen decency
yet haunts us. We ftumble and are impatient at the
leaft dividing of one vifible congregation from another,
though it be not in fundamentalls ; and through our
forwardnes to fuppreffe, and our backwardnes to recover any enthrall'd peece of truth out of the gripe of
cuftom, we care not to keep truth feparated from
truth, which is the fierceft rent and difunion of all.
We doe not fee that while we ftill affect by all means
a rigid externall formality, we may as foon fall again
into a groffe conforming ftupidity, a ftark and dead
congealment of *wood and hay and ftubble* forc't and
frozen together, which is more to the fudden degene-
rating of a Church then many *fubdichotomies* of petty
fchifms.   Not that I can think well of every light fepa-
ration, or that all in a Church is to be expected *gold
and filver and pretious ftones :* it is not poffible for man
to fever the wheat from the tares, the good fifh from
the other frie ; that muft be the Angels Miniftery at the
end of mortall things. Yet if all cannot be of one mind,
as who looks they fhould be ? this doubtles is more

wholfome, more prudent, and more Chriftian that many be tolerated, rather then all compell'd. I mean not tolerated Popery, and open fuperftition, which as it extirpats all religions and civill fupremacies, fo it felf fhould be extirpat, provided firft that all charitable and compaffionat means be us'd to win and regain the weak and mifled: that alfo which is impious or evil abfolutely either againft faith or maners no law can poffibly permit, that intends not to unlaw it felf: but thofe neighboring differences, or rather indifferences, are what I fpeak of, whether in fome point of doctrine or of difcipline, which though they may be many, yet need not interrupt *the unity of Spirit*, if we could but find among us *the bond of peace.* In the mean while if any one would write, and bring his helpfull hand to the flow-moving Reformation we labour under, if Truth have fpok'n to him before others, or but feem'd at leaft to fpeak, who hath fo bejefuited us that we fhould trouble that man with afking licence to doe fo worthy a deed? and not confider this, that if it come to prohibiting, there is not ought more likely to be prohibited then truth it felf; whofe firft appearance to our eyes blear'd and dimm'd with prejudice and cuftom, is more unfightly and unplaufible then many errors, ev'n as the perfon is of many a great man flight and contemptible to fee to. And what doe they tell us vainly of new opinions, when this very opinion of theirs, that none muft be heard, but whom they like, is the worft and neweft opinion of all others; and is the chief cause why fects and fchifms doe fo much abound, and true knowledge is kept at diftance from us; befides yet a greater danger which is in it. For when God fhakes a Kingdome with ftrong and health-full commotions to a generall reforming, 'tis not untrue that many fectaries and falfe teachers are then bufieft in feducing; but yet more true it is, that God then raifes to his own work men of rare abilities, and more then common induftry not only to look back and revife what hath bin taught heretofore, but to gain furder and goe on, fome new enlightn'd fteps in the difcovery of truth. For fuch is the order of Gods enlightning his Church, to difpenfe and deal out by degrees his beam, fo as our earthly eyes may beft fuftain it. Neither is God appointed and confin'd, where and out of what place thefe his chofen fhall be firft heard to fpeak; for he fees not as man fees, choofes not as man choofes, left we fhould devote our felves again to fet places, and affemblies, and outward callings of men ; planting our faith one while in the old Convocation houfe, and another while in the Chappell at Weftminfter; when all the faith and religion that fhall be there canoniz'd, is not fufficient without plain convincement, and the charity of patient inftruction to fupple the leaft bruife of confcience, to edifie the meaneft Chriftian, who de-fires to walk in the Spirit, and not in the letter of human truft, for all the number of voices that can be there made, no though *Harry* the 7. himfelf there, with all his leige tombs about him, fhould lend them voices from the dead, to fwell their number. And if the men be erroneous who appear to be the leading fchiimaticks, what witholds us but our floth, our felf-will, and diftruft in the right caufe, that we doe not give them gentle meetings and gentle dif-miffions, that we debate not and examin the matter throughly with liberall and frequent audience ; if not for their fakes, yet for our own? feeing no man who hath tafted learning, but will confeffe the many waies of profiting by thofe who not contented with ftale receits are able to manage, and fet forth new pofitions to the world. And were they but as the duft and cinders of our feet, fo long as in that notion they may ferve to polifh and brighten the armoury of Truth, ev'n for that refpect they were not utterly to be caft away. But if they be of thofe whom God hath fitted for the fpeciall ufe of thefe times with eminent and ample gifts, and thofe perhaps neither among the Priefts, nor among the Pharifees, and we in the haft of a precipitant zeal fhall make no diftinction, but refolve to ftop their mouths, becaufe we fear they come with new and dangerous opinions, as we commonly fore-judge them ere we underftand them, no leffe then woe to us, while thinking thus to defend the Gofpel, we are found the perfecutors.

There have bin not a few fince the beginning of this Parlament, both of the Prefbytery and others who by their unlicen't books to the contempt of an *Imprimatur* firft broke that triple ice clung about our hearts, and taught the people to fee day : I hope that none of thofe were the perfwaders to renew upon us this bondage which they themfelves have wrought fo much good by contemning. But if neither the check that *Mofes* gave to young *Jofhua*, nor the countermand which our Saviour gave to young *John*, who was fo ready to prohibit thofe whom he thought unlicenc't, be not anough to admonifh our Elders how unacceptable to God their tefty mood of prohibiting is, if neither their own remembrance what evill hath abounded in the Church by this lett of licencing, and what good they themfelves have begun by tranfgreffing it, be not anough, but that they will perfwade, and execute the moft *Dominican* part of the Inquifition over us, and are already with one foot in the ftirrup fo active at fuppreffing, it would be no unequall diftribution in the firft place to fuppreffe the fuppreffors themfelves ; whom the change of their condition hath puft up, more then their late experience of harder times hath made wife.

And as for regulating the Preffe, let no man think to have the honour of advifing ye better then your felves have done in that Order publifht next before this, that no book be Printed, unleffe the Printers and the Authors name, or at leaft the Printers be regifter'd.[6] Thofe which otherwife come forth, if they be found mifchievous and libellous, the fire and the executioner will be the timelieft and the moft effectuall remedy, that mans prevention can ufe. For this *authentic* Spanifh policy of licencing books, if I have faid ought, will prove the moft unlicenc't book it felf within a fhort while ; and was the immediat image of a Star-chamber decree[7] to that purpofe made in thofe very times when that Court did the reft of thofe her pious works, for which fhe is now fall'n from the Starres with *Lucifer*. Whereby ye may gueffe what kinde of State prudence, what love of the people, what care of Religion, or good manners there was at the contriving, although with fingular hypocrifie it pretended to bind books to their good behaviour. And how it got the upper hand of your precedent Order fo well conftituted before, if we may beleeve thofe men whofe profeffion gives them caufe to enquire moft, it may be doubted there was in it the fraud of fome old *patentees* and *monopolizers* in the trade of book-felling; who under pretence of the poor in their Company not to be defrauded, and the juft retaining of each man his feverall copy, which God forbid fhould be gainfaid, brought divers glofing colours to the Houfe, which were indeed but colours, and ferving to no end except it be to exercife a fuperiority over their neighbours, men who doe not therefore labour in an honeft profeffion to which learning is indetted, that they fhould be made other mens vaffals. Another end is thought was aym'd at by fome of them in procuring by petition this Order, that having power in their hands, malignant books might the eafier fcape abroad, as the event fhews. But of thefe *Sophifms* and *Elenchs* of marchandize I fkill not : This I know, that errors in a good government and in a bad are equally almoft incident ; for what Magiftrate may not be mif-inform'd, and much the fooner, if liberty of Printing be reduc't into the power of a few ; but to redreffe willingly and fpeedily what hath bin err'd, and in higheft autority to efteem a plain advertifement more then others have done a fumptuous bribe, is a vertue (honour'd Lords and Commons) anfwerable to Your higheft actions, and whereof none can participat but greateft and wifeft men.[8]

The End.

1. AREOPAGITICA—that which appertains to the Areopagus. There is at Athens a hill, formerly called ὸ Ἄρειος πάγος, 'the hill of Ares,' the 'Mar's Hill' of Acts xvii. 22, whereon ufed to affemble a Council, called 'The Council of the Areiopagus.' Befides fupreme judicial authority in cafes of wilful murder, this Council poffeffed very large focial influence ; having the general undefined fuperintendence of religion, morals, education, and the like. It was held in veneration by the whole people. It appears to have been ftrongly confervative in tone, and feems to have occupied a fomewhat fimilar pofition in the Athenian republic to that of the Houfe of Lords in the Britifh conftitution.

2. There were two Wardens in the Stationers' Company.

3. Reprinted at page 25.

4. BERNARDO DAVANZATI BOSTICHI [b. 30 Auguft 1529—d. 20 March 1606]. A Florentine author of confiderable repute. He wrote feveral works. I have not, as yet, been able to identify the particular one referred to by Milton.

5. ROBERT GREVIL, LORD BROOKE—The title of this book is, *A difcovrfe opening the natvre of that Epifcopacie, which is exercifed in England. Wherein, with all Humility, are reprefented fome Confiderations tending to the much-defired Peace, and long expected Reformation, of This our Mother Church.* By the Right Honourable ROBERT Lord BROOKE.—London, Printed by R. C. for *Samuel Cartwright*, and are to be fold at the figne of the Hand and Bible in Ducke-Lane 1641. This Lord Brooke was born in 1607, and was the fon of the celebrated Fulk Grevil, Lord Brooke of Beauchamps-court, the friend of Sir Philip Sidney. He was killed on 2 March 1642, while commanding the parliamentary forces attacking the Church-clofe at Litchfield. 'It fell ' out, that he having planted his great guns againft the South-' Eaft-gate of the Clofe, he was, tho' harneffed with plate-armour ' cap-a-pe, fhot from the church in the eye by one Diot, a ' Clergy-man's fon, (who could neither hear or fpeak) as he ftood ' in a door (whither he came to fee the occafion of a fudden ' fhout made by the foldiers) of which he inftantly died.'—A. à-Wood. *Athenæ Oxonienfes*, II. 433, Ed: by Blifs, 1815.

6. Reprinted at page 24.

7. Reprinted at page 7.

8. GILBERT MABBOTT, gentleman, was licenfer of pamphlets. He refigned on 22nd May, 1649, giving as his reafons arguments fimilar to those in the '*Areopagitica.*'

J. & W. Rider, Printers, London.